Cycling

Bicycling Mad

Beginner and Expert Strategies For Performing Better On Your Bike

By Ace McCloud
Copyright © 2016

Disclaimer

The information provided in this book is designed to provide helpful information on the subjects discussed. This book is not meant to be used, nor should it be used, to diagnose or treat any medical condition. For diagnosis or treatment of any medical problem, consult your own physician. The publisher and author are not responsible for any specific health or allergy needs that may require medical supervision and are not liable for any damages or negative consequences from any treatment, action, application or preparation, to any person reading or following the information in this book. Any references included are provided for informational purposes only. Readers should be aware that any websites or links listed in this book may change.

Table of Contents

DEDICATED TO THOSE WHO ARE PLAYING THE GAME OF LIFE TO

WIN

KEEP ON PUSHING AND NEVER GIVE UP!

Ace McCloud

Be sure to check out my website for all my Books and Audio books.

www.AcesEbooks.com

Introduction

I want to thank you and congratulate you for buying the book, "Cycling: Bicycling Made Easy: Beginner and Expert Strategies For Performing Better On Your Bike."

Cycling, also known as biking, is a great sport, a fun activity, and a practical mode of transportation. Many people regard cycling as a serious sport and work hard to succeed on the professional circuit. Others view it as a favorite pastime, taking bike rides along the beachfront or along nature trails just for fun. There are also a large number of people who depend on cycling as their primary mode of transportation, preferring the added maneuverability, or just desiring the exercise and fresh air.

There are many great benefits to cycling, whether you're training to be a pro, doing it for pure enjoyment, or biking to get from Point A to Point B. The greatest benefit is that it provides a powerful form of cardiovascular exercise and it strengthens core muscles as well as your legs. There is also the convenience; bicycles are easier to park and maneuver than cars and they can be ridden off-road, they are easily stored, and are quickly set into motion.

Cycling is also environmentally friendly. Bikes consume no fossil fuels, they neither contribute to noise pollution nor increase air pollution. They cause no damage to roadways and they cost next to nothing to maintain. Bikes are easily transported, often fitting easily inside a larger vehicle. For smaller cars, racks and bike holders will firmly attach your two-wheeler to the top or back of your vehicle. If you employ public transportation, you will find special accommodations for stashing your bike on buses and trains. The only disadvantages to cycling are the possible stresses on your body from the exertion of a long ride and, depending on where you live, the difficulties presented by the local weather or traffic conditions.

Whether you want to develop a professional cycling career, or just want to ride for the sheer pleasure of it, this book is for you. It contains proven steps and strategies on how to become a better bike rider. Here you will discover the best information and tips that can help you become an expert cyclist! From gear and equipment that will optimize your ride to tips on priming your body to get the most out of the experience, there is something in this book for pretty much everyone.

You will also discover the best strategies and techniques that you can easily apply to become a top cyclist, followed by the best diet and strength training programs you can engage in to build a powerful cycling physique. Easy-to-understand instructions walk you through the stretching and warm-up exercises that will help protect your body from injuries that are common among cyclists.

You will also be able to choose from the top five best workouts for cyclists as well as learn how to design a custom workout based on your own personal needs.

Also included are inspirational stories and the best mental techniques you can utilize to hone your mind to a sharp an edge! By using your favorite strategies contained in this book, you can put everything together to improve your cycling skills and climb to the top at a rapid pace!

Chapter 1: Gearing Up For the Road

Like any sport, cycling requires some essential equipment to help keep you safe, healthy, and prepared for any situation. Though the list of gear for this sport is not as exhaustive as for football or baseball, it is critical to have the right kind of equipment for the conditions under which you'll be riding. This chapter will help you become prepared with the right equipment the next time you decide to hop on your bike and take it out for a spin!

Your Helmet

The most important piece of gear you will need for cycling, hands down, is your helmet! Wearing a helmet can easily prevent a small knock on the noggin from becoming a dangerous concussion.

I'll never forget when I got my first bike. I was five years old and it was one of the things I received for Christmas that year, along with a matching helmet. My mother wouldn't let me out of her sight with that bike until she saw I was wearing my helmet. It was a good thing, too, as I've taken many a spill since, but the helmet has always been there to save my skull, often quite literally.

In 2012, I was on a vacation in Maui, Hawaii on a bike tour. A group of us tourists took the easy route, riding up Haleakala Summit (a mountain that soars 10,000 feet into the sky) in a van that dropped us off at the peak so we could coast back down on our bikes. Before we left, they gave us some equipment for the trip that included a full-face helmet.

It had been a while since I had done any serious bike riding and I had no idea how steep that mountainside would be! I wasn't on the bike for five minutes before I veered into oncoming traffic and had to make a split-second decision between going over the edge and running head-on into a car. I chose to go over the edge, where luckily my 20-foot fall was broken by a tree. I injured my shoulder and knee and my nose got banged up pretty badly, but imagine if I hadn't been wearing my helmet – I would have more than likely incurred serious injury if I wasn't killed outright on the spot!

I can't warn you strongly enough: WEAR YOUR HELMET! It is easy to think "That will never happen to me," but believe me, it can!

Helmets are available wherever bicycles are sold: sporting goods stores, big box stores, and even the internet. I highly suggest you fork over the money to get a safe helmet. Look for helmets certified by the CPS. Don't sacrifice safety for aesthetic appeal.

While many of the helmets on the market come with cool, colorful designs, you'll want to make sure that they also come with a nice, hard top that will protect your head in the event of an accident. You'll also want a helmet that fits your head snugly; a loose helmet can shift, compromising your vision as well as failing to adequately protect your cranium.

Before parting with your well-earned cash, check online for user recommendations and feedback to see what works best for others. If you can, avail yourself of the advice of the pros at your local bike shop; they can ensure you get the best fit for the price.

Proper Footwear

Since people commonly engage in cycling during warmer weather, the temptation is to wear open-toed shoes, flip-flops, or sandals. Even though advertisers like to film people pedaling along the beach in flip flops or barefoot, don't do this! Riding without the proper footwear can cause a slew of problems. First, thin or absent footwear doesn't support your foot; you can suffer strains, burst blisters, or even find it difficult to keep your feet on the pedals. Second, if your foot slips into the spokes or gets caught in the chain, we're talking major pain, and possibly a trip to the emergency room.

It's just an overall bad idea. I, too, have learned this for myself. Remember the bike I got when I was five years old? I often rode wearing nothing but sandals. I can still feel the searing pain from stubbed toes and the scraped feet I got from the spills I took on the gravel driveway in my backyard. Ouch!

The best footwear for casual cycling is sneakers. Even if you are on vacation at the beach and you're wearing flip flops, toss an old pair of sneakers into your bag, just in case. Specialty biking calls for more specific footwear. A mountain biker will probably wear shoes designed with a stiff sole for efficient pedaling and a rubber-lug sole with recessed cleats for walking on vigorous terrain. Other footwear comes with cleats that attach to the pedals of your bike to maximize the effectiveness of your pedal stroke. Some also come with extra features like waterproof linings or extra ankle protection.

When choosing your footwear, you'll want something that provides a snug heel fit with ample toe room and comfortable support. Your shoes should leave enough room for your toes to move around in the front but should not slip on your heel. While they will feel stiff at first, the shoes will mold better to your feet over time.

It is important to properly maintain your biking footwear. Many companies sell accessories such as blow dryers and shoe and toe covers and other cleaning supplies. When your cleats begin to disengage from your pedal or if they break or crack, it is time for a replacement. Look for replacement cleats that match your existing ones. Bring your pedal into the bike shop with you to make sure the cleats fit, and don't hesitate to ask for help; that's why the experts work there.

The Saddle

Because you'll be spending a lot of time "in the saddle", this is one piece of equipment you want to be sure you're comfortable with. There is nothing worse than being perched atop a torture device for hours at a time.

If you've just purchased a bike and find that sitting on it is uncomfortable, don't jump right out and purchase a new seat right away; try adjusting it first. The most common problem is that your seat is just too high. At the wrong height, your body is forced to shift back and forth to work the pedals, increasing your discomfort.

You should be able to sit on your bike with your hips level and make no changes as you pedal to the bottom of your stroke. If you can't reach the bottom of your stroke without adjusting your hips, your seat is too high. On the other hand, if your knee is still bent at the bottom of your stroke, you will want to raise your seat.

Your seat height matters. When I got my first bike at age five, it came with training wheels. When I asked to have them removed so I could ride like the other kids, I ran into trouble. Learning to ride without training wheels was one of the toughest challenges I had ever faced. No matter what, I just couldn't persuade that bike to stay upright! Fortunately, my grandfather eventually realized my seat was way too high for my little legs. All it took was a simple height adjustment and I was riding steadily in no time.

In addition to height, the angle of your seat may need adjusting. Most bikes come with a clamp right under the seat itself. All you do is loosen the screw until you can tilt the seat to your liking. Often, a slight downward tilt in front can make a huge difference. Just be sure you tighten that screw before you ride off again. Most seats can also be slid forward or backward to ensure that your legs are directly above the pedals.

If none of these adjustments work for you, then you will most likely benefit from purchasing an entirely new seat. If you're riding recreationally, a **cushioning seat** may be the best solution. This type of seat is designed for short-term biking and comes with wide, soft padding for your backside. It even looks comfortable.

A **performance seat** is best for those who race, tour or take trips of multiple days on their bikes. This type of seat is long and narrow, supporting your hips without interfering with your legs as they constantly spin along. Mountain bikers may prefer a **mountain-specific seat** due to the variety of positions they find themselves in on the trails. Because women tend to have wider hips than men, it's also easy to find seats designed specifically for women.

An alternative to buying a seat is to try a cushioning pad that fits over your seat. There are two main type of seat cushions for bikes: **gel** and **foam**. Gel cushioning, like memory foams, conforms to your body and provides a comfortable ride for recreational riders. The negative aspect of gel cushioning is that it can easily stiffen from excessive pressure. Foam cushioning is much more flexible than gel cushioning; it is firm and easily molds back into shape. Foam cushioning is generally preferred by long-distance cyclists and individuals who weigh more than 200 pounds.

Reflective Clothing

Bright colors and reflective clothing can be a literal life-saver, especially if you're on the road at night. Bikers, because of their relatively small size, can be almost invisible once the sun sets. Since most towns don't allow bikers to ride on sidewalks, you will often have to share the same road all the cars and semis out there. In the majority of car vs. bike accidents, drivers said they didn't see the biker until it was too late. For this reason, you should do everything you can to make yourself visible when you ride. Avoid dark colors. Instead, opt for white or bright yellow, especially for your shirt, because it will be the most visible part of your anatomy.

Wear a reflective vest; I recommend carrying one with you, just in case you find yourself on the road after sunset. I also recommend using a bike light; as a kid I used one that generated light as I pedaled, but LED battery-powered lights are easily obtainable today. A light, in addition to making your visible to traffic can illuminate obstacles in your path that you otherwise would not see in the dark.

Weather Gear

Since you'll do most of your biking outdoors, you need to be prepared for all types of weather. Rain is often most common, but you can easily protect yourself with a durable poncho. Ponchos can be folded down to make for easy toting and they also usually come in bright colors so nobody on the road will overlook you in the reduced visibility. To keep your head dry, you can use a hooded poncho. You'll also want a pair of gloves to protect your hands in cold or wet weather. Find a pair that fits snugly and that has a waterproof lining.

If you're biking in cold weather, you have several options for your head. Some helmets come with a cover that is adequate for cold days. Bikers often generate enough heat that they don't need further head insulation, but if anything is needed, a skull cap or a balaclava worn under the helmet should be sufficient.

If you're biking in hot, sunny weather, put on some sunscreen 30 minutes before you head out. Reapply sunscreen every few hours to keep yourself well protected. I also recommend sunglasses, not just for the sun, but also to protect your eyes from dust, bugs, and flying debris.

Hydration

Since cycling is a physically intense sport, it is essential to stay hydrated when you ride. Water is crucial for your body's performance and you will lose plenty as you sweat. The best hydration schedule is to drink 20 ounces of water for every hour of riding. You may need to adjust your water intake depending on the weather conditions. If you're biking in hot weather and sweating profusely, you may need to drink more. Always drink something every hour, even if you're not thirsty, to avoid dehydration.

You can transport your water in a basic water bottle but you can also buy a **hydration pack** for greater water storage. A hydration pack is like a backpack with a bladder that holds water you can conveniently sip through an attached hose. Hydration packs are beneficial because of the extra storage and the fact that you won't need to stop to replenish your water supply. Research shows that bikers who carry hydration packs tend to get better hydration than those who just carry water bottles.

Your Bike

Of course the equipment that makes cycling possible is your bike itself. The size of your bicycle frame and the relationship between the pedals, the placement of your cleats, the positioning of your seat, and your handlebar setup can make all the difference between a pleasant ride and one that leaves you crippled in pain hours later.

The vast majority of cycling injuries – not counting the broken bones, scrapes and tears that come from crashing – are caused by either overuse or improper positioning of the body on the bicycle. Because cycling is a highly repetitive activity, many aches, pains, and much discomfort can be traced back to how you ride, that is, the way your body moves as you pedal and your general posture on the bike. For that reason, pay attention to your body. It complains for a reason.

If you start hurting – beyond the normal aches and pains of training – look for the part of your bike that might be contributing to the problem and see if a minor tweak makes a difference. If your hands start to go numb, for example, shift the way you hold the handlebars, lighten your grip, or adjust the handlebars themselves to see if you can alleviate the problem. If your knees begin hurting, check into both the positioning of your seat and the set of your cleats and how you pedal.

Don't just keep on riding day after day if the pain doesn't improve. There's no need to cause permanent damage; after all, you started cycling because you enjoy it, not as a form of torture. If you can't fix the problem by making adjustments, especially if giving your body some recovery time doesn't help, it may be time to visit a doctor.

Chapter 2: Stretching, Warm-up, And Cool-Down Techniques for Cyclists

Cycling is like any other aerobic sport in that you need to both ramp up as you begin and ramp down your activity level before you stop. This is easy to overlook in the desire to hit the road, but your body will serve you better in the long run if you pay attention to the information and practical tips in this chapter

Stretching Helps

Stretching is an important activity to incorporate into your daily routine. It is especially important for cyclists because biking can cause tightness in your lower body due to the repetitive nature of the motions inherent in pedaling. Smart cyclists stretch before and after riding, incorporating targeted stretches into both their warm-ups and their cool-downs. Stretching can help keep your muscles flexible and strong, enabling you to sustain an active lifestyle. It can also improve your posture, balance, and coordination, all of which are necessary if you want to enjoy your bike outings.

Failure to stretch can result in tears or strains; lack of stretching can lead to very painful injuries that sideline you while you heal. Not stretching can contribute to poor circulation, reduced range of motion, and chronic muscle soreness, each of which can block your progress toward cycling proficiency.

Many of the common cycling injuries – both those caused by posture and injuries due to over-use – can be minimized, if not outright prevented, by regular stretching. If you adopt the habit of stretching, you will find any injuries you do receive will respond much better to healing treatments.

Warm Up First

Warming up helps your body in several ways. First, it increases the amount of blood flow to your heart and other muscles, which helps prepare them for an increased work load. It also boosts the amount of oxygen and nutrients that are sent to your muscles. A good warm-up will lubricate your joints, readying them for activity and can help you mentally prepare to work your body by boosting your energy level and upping your enthusiasm.

To start your warm-up you want to engage in **light aerobics**. This could include a brisk walk, a slow jog, or a spin on a stationary bike. You could also march in place, walk up and down a flight of stairs, bounce on a mini trampoline, take a swim or engage in any other activity that gets your heart pumping.

Dynamic Stretches

Once you've finished your light aerobic activity, you can complete a light dynamic stretching routine to continue warming up your muscles. The following dynamic routine will both engage your cardiovascular system and continue to engage your muscles:

Note: when a description below mentions only one side of your body, perform it on the other side as well. Your objective is to reach balanced flexibility

Prisoner Squats: Stand with your feet slightly farther apart than your shoulders. Place your hands behind your head. Lower your body into a squat and look upward. Squat down as far as possible without bending your knees any further. Hold that position for a moment and then push yourself back up. For additional force building, you can propel yourself up off the ground when you push back up if you choose.

Jump Rope: Rapidly jump up and down while quickly twirling a jump rope underneath your feet. Spring up from the ground using primarily your feet and ankles.

Jumping Jacks: Stand with your feet together and your arms at rest by your sides. Keeping both arms and legs relatively straight, jump up while widening your stance and raising your arms away from your sides to higher than your shoulders. Jump up a second time, returning both feet and hands to their original position Repeat this motion without pause until you feel your heart pumping.

Ankle Bounces: Rapidly jump and up and down, springing off the floor with your feet and ankles.

Walking Lunges: Stand tall with your feet shoulder-width apart. Step forward into a lunge and bend both knees to lower your hips to the ground. Avoid touching your back knee to the ground. Shift your weight onto your forward foot and use your back foot to push off the ground; bring your back leg forward and step into another lunge.

Side Step Lunge: Stand upright with your feet slightly apart and your knees slightly bent. Keeping your left knee and aligned above your left toes, step directly to your left. While your weight is still on your left leg, bring your right foot leftward until you have returned to the starting posture. Repeat several times to the left, then reverse the lunge, stepping to the right.

Toe Touches: Stand upright with your feet shoulder distance apart. Bend at the waist, allowing your arms to hang down as you lower your upper body headfirst. Relax and allow your arms and torso to naturally hang in front of your legs for 2 seconds before rising to your original position.

Power Skips: Skip rapidly as high and as far forward as you can.

Arm Circles: Stand upright with your legs shoulder-width apart, holding your arms out to each side, palms facing forward. Begin swinging your arms in small circles for at least 10 seconds. Stop and repeat, circling your arms in the opposite direction.

Crunches: lie on your back on the floor. Place your hands together behind your head. Without bending your neck, raise your torso until your shoulder blades come up off the floor. Lower yourself to the starting position and repeat multiple times.

Lateral Leg Swings: Stand with a wall or other support to your right, touching it with your hand as needed for balance. Lift your left foot about an inch off the ground. Swing the left leg out (to the left) and back 10 times. Turn around and repeat the process with your right leg.

Pendulum Swings: Stand a couple feet behind a chair back with your legs shoulder width apart. Keeping a straight back and bending your knees slightly, lean forward at the waist and grasp the top of the chair with your right hand. Let your left arm hang loose from the shoulder socket. Using your upper body to start the motion, swing the left arm back and forth, both from side to side, front to back, and in a circular motion, about 10 times each. Then, repeat this exercise with your right arm.

Shoulder Rolls: While seated on a chair, rest your hands on your legs. Breathe in and roll your shoulders backward, up, forward and down as you breathe out. Let your shoulders rest, then take another deep breath in and roll your shoulders the opposite direction as you breathe out.

Running in Place: Run in place for one minute, lifting your knees high.

Single Leg Hops: Stand on your left leg, behind a marker of some sort. Flex your knee, then jump forward over the marker, landing on your left leg. You can set up multiple markers for a multiple-hop exercise if you want. Remember to repeat on the right leg.

Standing Hip Circles: Balance on your left leg, with your left hand holding onto something for support. Raise your right knee up to a 90 degree angle and draw a circle in the air with it. This allows you to open up your hips. Draw a circle in the opposite direction, then put your foot down.

Paulwebb.tv has put together a video containing a really good stretching warm up routine, called Full Body Dynamic Warm Up. It will demonstrate most of these exercises.

Static Stretching

The remaining stretches in this chapter are in a special category; they are called static stretches because you hold a specific position for a period of time. Your body needs these stretches, don't get me wrong. Just be careful when you perform them. **Because static stretches have been found to reduce your power output for up to an hour following their use, you should <u>never</u> perform these exercises right before you ride.**

Lower Body Stretches

Here are some of the best stretches for the muscles in your legs. The muscle groups we'll target here are your hamstrings, quadriceps, calf muscles, and glutes

Standing Quadriceps Stretch (10 to 30 seconds per leg) – Stand straight with your right hand against a wall for support; then bend your left foot behind you. Take your left hand and pull your heel to your buttocks. Stand straight and continue to pull your foot up until you feel the stretch in your thigh.

Seated Hamstring Stretch (10 to 30 seconds) – Sit on the floor and stretch your legs out in front of you. Keeping your knees straight, reach your arms forward as you bend at your waist.

Standing Calf Stretch (10 to 30 seconds per leg) – Stand facing a wall, one step behind it. Step forward with your left leg. Pressing your right heel into the ground, lower your body and keep your back leg straight as you lean against the wall. Lower yourself until you can feel a stretch.

Hip Flexor Stretch (10 to 30 seconds) – This stretch will work your hip flexors. Lie down on the floor and bend your knees over your upper body like a baby. Use both hands to grasp your feet between your knees and feel the stretch.

Hip Flexor Stretch 2 (10 to 30 seconds) – Sit on the floor and straighten out your legs before you. Breathe in and bend your left knee, putting the sole of your left foot against the top of your right inner thigh. Keeping both hips firmly on the floor, breathe in as you reach your right arm straight up and then forward, breathing out as you lower your arm and let your hand land naturally on your right leg. Slowly bend your right shoulder down toward your right knee, allowing your right elbow to lower to the floor inside your leg until you feel a stretch.

Plantar Fasciitis Stretch (10 to 30 seconds per foot) – Sit in a chair and cross your left leg over your right ankle. Grasp your toes just above the ball of your foot and pull them back until you feel a stretch in the bottom of your heel.

Achilles Stretch (10 to 30 seconds per foot) – Stand facing a wall, one step behind it. Step forward with your left leg. Pressing your right heel into the ground, lower your body and keep your back leg straight as you lean toward the wall. Lower yourself toward the wall until you can feel a stretch.

Upper Body Stretches

It is also important to stretch your chest and shoulders. Since you will spend much of your time with your upper body bent over your handlebars, it is important to counter your body's tendency to shorten those muscles that would otherwise eventually leave your back hunched over a caved-in chest.

Shoulder Stretch (10 to 30 seconds per arm) – Sit on a chair. Raise your right arm, bending it at the elbow behind your head so that your hand stretches down the center of your back. Use your left hand to grasp your wrist and pull it downwards until a stretch occurs in your triceps and shoulders. If you cannot reach your wrist you can simply pull your arm back from below the elbow. An alternative is to grasp a towel in your right hand, letting it fall down your back for the left hand to grab and pull downward.

Chest Stretch (10 to 30 seconds) – Stand straight with your feet shoulder width apart and your chest high. Extend both arms straight out from your sides with your palms facing the floor. Move your arms as far back as you can until a stretch occurs in your chest.

Camel Pose (5 breaths) – Get down on your knees, placing them at least two fist widths apart. Place your hands on your lower back. Tighten your abdomen and tip your tailbone down. Gazing toward the far wall, lift your chest up and squeeze your shoulder blades together.

Whole-Body Stretches

Your body needs these stretches both to engage muscles that haven't otherwise been targeted and to program your body to balance the use of multiple muscles.

Downward Facing Dog (5 breaths) – Get down on all fours. Inhale as you relax your upper back and straighten your elbows. Exhale, extending your hips upward, and straightening your legs to form an upside down "V" shape. Relax your head and let it hang down between your arms.

Runner's Lunge (10 to 30 seconds per leg) – Stand straight and inhale. Exhale as you step forward with your right foot into a lunge position and lower your body until your fingers can make contact with the ground. Inhale as you straighten out your right leg. Exhale as you slowly return to the lunge position and then back to your starting position. Repeat this stretch four times on each leg.

Bridge Pose (5 breaths) – Lie down on your back. Bend your knees and place your feet on the floor with your heels against your hips. Placing your hands by your sides for stability, raise your hips off the floor. As your hips rise, lift your chest also keeping your back straight.

Lower Back Stretch (10 to 30 seconds) – Sit on the floor and bend your knees, keeping your feet on the ground. Use your hands to pull your chest toward your knees.

You will find it much safer to start cycling after completing this stretching routine. Once you are finished cycling for the day, it is equally important to follow a cool down routine to ensure that you will protect your muscles even further. To cool down you can simply repeat some of the dynamic stretches from your warm-up routine. The most important areas to focus on when cooling down are your lower legs, thighs, hips and lower back.

Chapter 3: How to Be a Better Cyclist

In this chapter I've addressed a wide range of topics that can affect your cycling effectiveness, for better or for worse. You will find here some of the best tips and strategies for workouts, safety issues, performance measurement and motivation as well as techniques on how to build your cycling skills.

Invest Time

The first thing to accept about cycling is that it's a time investment. Most professionals will attribute their success to all the time they spent on their bike. To improve as a cyclist you will be spending training time both on your bike and off it. Success does not come overnight; it can take years to become a great cyclist. However, as long as you are willing to invest the time, commit to continuous improvement, and embrace biking opportunities, you will remain on the path to success.

Start Slow

It can take some time for your body to grow used to cycling; the sport works muscles you may not use as part of your everyday life. Don't push too hard, or you'll lose your enjoyment of the sport and risk injuries. This is a sport of the long haul. Don't rush your training; nothing happens overnight.

Start off slowly and only step up your riding after your body says it's ready. For example, start off by completing a one-mile ride, but don't increase the distance until you are able to complete the one mile with energy to spare.

The same rule applies to physical training. Carefully schedule your workouts to avoid over-training any one muscle group and to ensure adequate recovery time between workouts.

Join a Cycling Group

Cycling groups offer opportunities to learn more about riding by watching and learning from more experienced cyclists. They're also great places for social interaction. Many riders find greater accountability within groups as well as more enjoyment in the companionship of group rides and training.

Ride With Those Who Are Fast

To push yourself to grow, pair yourself part of the time with cyclists who are faster than you. You can do this in a cycling group or among your own group of friends. By riding with those who are faster, you are challenging yourself to keep up with them; before you know it, your speed and endurance will have improved.

Switch up Ride Intensities

Many cyclists fall into the habit of riding at a slow and steady pace. This doesn't really do much to get the heart pumping, nor does it increase your stamina. Riding at one pace for too long can actually train your body to only go at that pace. To boost your abilities, switch up your riding intensities. Take routes that will challenge you to work harder. Ride with friends you know will set a faster pace. Then surprise your body with an easy ride before ratcheting up the difficulty level again. The variety will prompt your body to build more fast-twitch muscle fibers to allow you to pedal at a more intense rate when necessary.

Measure Your Progress

Don't just guess at how you're doing. Objective measurements let you know that your training is working and can warn you when you're working too hard and need to give your body a rest. When you've think you've reached peak performance, measurable results will let you see just how much further you can push yourself. Measuring your results can also point out areas where you can focus your training for additional growth.

The simplest measurement of your abilities is to calculate the time it takes to ride a specific route. Every six weeks or so, calculate your time on that route and compare it to your previous measurements.

Invest in a Bike Computer

A bike computer is similar to a FitBit. You can attach it to your bike and it will measure statistics such as how fast and how far you've travelled, your current RPMs, etc. A bike computer is not essential, but it can definitely prove useful if you're looking for data to help you track your progress.

Log Your Rides and Workouts

One way to track your progress is to log your rides and workouts. This gives you a visible measurement of where you are compared to where you want to be. Logging these items may seem tedious at first but it can become easier as you get used to it. Keep your logs filled out completely and accurately. It's not necessary to share them with anyone else, but honesty is important, especially if you want an accurate record of your progress.

Use Time Trials

Time trials are known as "the race of truth" because, as a single-person race, there is nobody to draft behind and no group to support you. You're on your own.

Participants run a set course by themselves, with cyclists hitting the starting line thirty seconds apart. A time trial can increase your discomfort immunity, as you will be focused on pushing yourself for a set amount of miles. Most cycling groups schedule time trials periodically and can help you prepare for the race. Time trials can help you build speed, endurance, and readiness for your next challenging ride.

Apply The 80/20 Rule To Training

The 80/20 rule states that you should focus on the 20% responsible for 80% of your achievements. This principle can be applied to almost anything, including your training. The best way to apply the 80/20 rule to your training is to review your training for the previous year. Think about what you did prior to having a really successful race or an overall good feeling about cycling. Take whatever it was and focus on that to keep building your strength, power, and confidence.

Review Your Sleep Schedule

Healthy sleep habits can wield a huge impact on your performance. Sleep allows your body to recharge and your mind to prepare for the next day. Without it, your physical and mental performance can drastically decline. When you sleep, your body goes to work to repair the damage you inflicted upon it during the day, so be sure to get a good night's slumber after a hard training session.

It almost goes without saying that cycling on little to no sleep can be dangerous. A sleep-deprived mind is befuddled enough to miss signs of unstable road surfaces or other dangers. You can easily end up in collisions or wipe-outs.

Here are some tips to optimize your sleeping habits:

- Sleep on the right stuff. Your pillow should be firm enough to support your head and keep your neck in a straight line with the rest of your spine. Use a non-allergenic pillow and wash the pillowcase regularly to minimize your exposure to bacteria, allergens, and mold. Your bed should be firm enough to support your body, keeping your spine straight.

- Expose yourself to plenty of natural light during the day. Open your shades as soon as you wake up to let the sun shine through. Spend as much time as you can outdoors or near windows.

- Reduce your stimulant exposure at night. About one hour before you go to bed, you should begin to wean yourself off of all electronics. Yes, this means it's time to turn off the television, put your computer to sleep and stop playing games on your phone. This signals your body that it's time to wind down for the night.

  When it's triggered by a decrease in light, your body steps up its production of melatonin, a natural sleep hormone Too much of the wrong kind of light can hinder melatonin production, leaving you wide awake when you should be dozing off.

- It's okay to read a relaxing book before bed; just make it a real, physical book, not an e-reader. While you're at it, dim the background lights, switch to soothing music at a low volume and, definitely, cut out the caffeine.

Safety First

As a cyclist, safety should be your number one priority. The roads are dangerous; one in every 41 auto accidents involves a cyclist. Learn your city's bicycle laws and observe them, as well as practicing basic common sense. While you're tooling down the road amid cars and pedestrians, here are a few things to watch for:

- A car door opening. Watch for tail-lights to switch off, an indication that the engine has been cut, the car is in park, and the driver may be exiting soon.

- A person or animal stepping in front of you. This is most likely when entering an intersection, but it is also possible for pedestrians to cross the street between stopped vehicles. Keep alert and pay attention to where the pedestrians and animals are in your vicinity.

- A car pulling into your path. Watch parked cars for engine lights, turn signals, or other indications that a driver may be thinking of pulling into traffic.

- A car turning in front of you. Don't pass cars on the right when they slow down; they may be preparing to turn right and you don't want to be there when they do!

- For that matter, don't pass cars on the left when they slow down, either. They could be preparing to turn left. You'd best keep to your lane.

Precautionary Measures

- Turn on your front and rear lights. This is most essential at night, but can also serve to alert oncoming drivers during the day.

- Wave your arm if a vehicle appears to be coming right toward you. Sometimes the movement will attract a driver's attention, but be prepared for evasive maneuvers, just in case.

- Wear light-colored clothing.

- Wear reflective gear, on your helmet, jacket, shoes, etc.

- If your local laws permit, ride on the sidewalk instead of the street. Just be courteous and yield to pedestrians when you are on a walkway.

- Avoid being boxed in by traffic. Know where all vehicles are at all times and have an escape plan to avoid being crushed in the middle of a group of those thousand-pound behemoths.

- Never ride against traffic. It is potentially confusing to drivers and is usually illegal.

- Never pull up to the right of a car at a stop light. Wait behind it until the light turns green.

- Stop for red lights. Don't even think of riding through an intersection before the light turns green!

In general, it is best to avoid busy streets if possible and use hand signals. Point your arm out to the left to make a left turn. You can do the same with your right arm to make a right turn. Do not ride with headphones and stay alert to your surroundings at all times.

Check Your Tire Pressure

If your tires are under- or over-inflated, they can slow you down. Carry a pressure gauge with you and check your tires periodically. Tire pressure can vary, based on changes in temperature and humidity.

Know How To Fix A Flat

The most common problem you will probably encounter while on your bike is the event of a flat tire. Practice at home, both taking off your back and front wheels as well as removing and replacing an inner tube. You should know how to replace a tire before you hit the road. Carry a pump, a patch kit and a spare tube with you at all times. If you experience a flat tire and are without a spare inner tube, here are the steps to repair it:

1. Take the wheel off the bike. Look for anything protruding from the tire, or any other indicators showing the location of the leak.

2. remove the tire from the wheel and extract the inner tube.

3. Pump some air into the tube and listen for the hissing sound of air escaping in order to locate the hole.

4. Use the sandpaper from your patch kit to scratch over the hole. The area you scratch should be a little bigger than the patch you're going to use.

5. Spread a thin layer of glue, also part of your patch kit, over the sanded area. Place the patch over the glued area and hold it together for about 30 seconds. The glue should dry almost instantly.

6. Before replacing the tire, inspect it carefully, extracting any rocks, thorns, glass, or other foreign objects that could cause further damage. After you've eyeballed the outside, run your fingers along the inside of the tire to catch anything else that is poking through.

7. Now look at the tire rim for any spoke ends protruding through the rim tape. If you find a spot, affix a small patch to the area and get the rim looked at after you get home.

8. First put one side of the tire back onto the rim. Pump a little air into the tube just so it isn't completely flabby, then insert the new tube into the tire.

9. After the inner tube is fully inserted, put the rest of the tire back on the rim. Once the tire is completely reinstalled, pump it up and ride on!

Value Strength Training

Many cyclists avoid strength training because they are afraid it will add unnecessary pounds to their frame. However, strength training is very important, especially for your leg muscles; they are your main source of power.

While it is true that you should avoid gaining body weight, it is possible to build power into your muscles without adding unnecessary pounds. You will learn more about proper strength training in a few chapters.

Increase Your Speed

Speed is an important factor in cycling because it generally determines where you will rank compared to other cyclists. It's also natural to wonder how fast you're going and how much faster you can get. Here are a few tips that can help you increase your speed:

- Minimize your wind resistance. Wind resistance is the greatest physical hindrance to speed. By bending and tucking your elbows in toward your body, you will naturally lower your profile, making it more aerodynamic.

  To test this, start out by cycling with your body fully upright and then switch to the new position and you'll be shocked by the immediate difference.

- Wear snug clothing when you're biking outdoors. Loose clothing can easily catch the wind and slow you down. Snug clothing can also help you stay cool and dry as it wicks moisture from your body.

- Pay attention to your pedaling speed and your gear selection. Both have a direct relationship to how fast you move forward.

Listen To Music

Experts recommend that outdoor cyclists avoid wearing headphones for safety reasons, so limit this to when you're training indoors. Research shows that listening to music while you cycle can help your body ignore tiredness, muscle soreness, and that burning sensation in your lungs. Listening to music can help you pedal harder and faster without noticing the extra exertion. Choose music tempos that match their beat with your optimum pedal stroke speed.

Boost Your Climbing Skills

Climbing is an important skill for cyclists because, face it, life is a series of hills and valleys. Climbing skills are essential to becoming a great cyclist. The primary muscle used in climbing is your glutes. If your gluteal muscles are not strong enough, you will end up over-using your quads and hamstrings for power. This can result in a strength imbalance that may leave your lower legs fatigued when you really need them. A great way to keep your glutes strong and active is – you guessed it – exercises! Here are a couple exercises designed to enhance your glute strength:

1. **Single Leg Box Jump:** This exercise will require a box or another; sturdy surface you can jump onto. It should be at least 10 inches high. Stand on one leg and jump onto the surface. Land on the leg you jumped with. As soon as you land, jump back down. Perform this exercise 12 times for each leg.

2. **Glute/Hamstring Raise:** This exercise requires the assistance of a partner. Lie face down on the ground and ask your partner to hold your legs against the floor. Contract your hamstring muscles and lift your body up until you're in a kneeling position. Slowly lower yourself back to the floor. Focus on using your hamstrings to get your body off the floor and use your glutes to complete the motion.

Increase Pedaling Efficiency

While pedaling a bike is very simple, there is a whole science to mastering the spin. It entails a much smaller range of motion than many other sports, but there is an art to effective pedaling. Many cyclists make the mistake of pushing their foot straight down when the pedal is at the top of its revolution. The only time you should be pushing your foot straight down is when your foot and the pedal are in the three o'clock position, nearest to the front of the bicycle. If you push your foot straight down throughout the entire motion, you will be wasting the power of your quads.

Fast pedaling can reduce the force placed on your quadriceps by transferring some of it to your heart and lungs. This is a good thing, because your heart and lung tissue can regenerate faster than the muscle tissue in your quadriceps.

To master your pedal stroke, there are a few things to keep in mind. The most important part of the stroke is at the top and bottom. The other parts of your stroke move so quickly that it can be difficult to focus on them. Anticipate the upward motion of the pedal when it's at the bottom, and its shift to downward motion when it approaches the top. When your foot passes the upright, you're your feet forward to induce power.

You can increase your pedaling skills with targeted pedaling exercises I'll describe later and by riding off-road. Off-road terrain requires a perfect pedal stroke because you are working to keep traction between your tires and the terrain.

Ankling To The Rescue

When we talk about pedaling, we usually focus on the power stroke downward and just give the leg a free ride on the up-stroke. However, have you ever tried to add power to your stroke by pulling up as you return to the top of the pedal revolution? The technique's name comes from the flexing in your ankle as you adjust the angle of your foot throughout the pedaling cycle. While not everyone is an ankling advocate, enough cyclists have reported experiencing improved efficiencies and less muscle fatigue through this technique that it is worth your consideration.

Ankling works best when you are pedaling at a medium cadence, between 60 and 110 revolutions per minute. Any faster makes it difficult to consciously adjust the tilt of the pedal. This technique can reap the greatest benefits when climbing hills, although it is also useful when cycling on the flat.

The technique is perfectly safe, as long as your cleats and your seat height are set appropriately. Do not expect your ankling to look just like a friend's; the amount of flex in your ankle is a function of genetics and physical flexibility. As always, if you experience any pain when ankling, stop immediately and have these settings checked by an expert before cycling further.

Get A Handle On Braking

Braking is important for safety. Braking too hard can cause injuries, just as surely as inadequate braking. The only way to really learn is to use your brakes, but I can provide some guidelines that will get you started.

Most bikes have both front and rear brakes and you will need to know when to use which and in what ratios. Beginners often utilize both brakes to bring their bike to a stop but many experienced cyclists can safely stop using the front brakes alone. Once you've learned how to safely stop with your front brakes, you should save your rear brakes only for situations in which the ground you're riding on has no traction, or in a situation where a tire blows out.

You also need to learn how to use your front brake when you need to make an emergency stop. Using your rear brake will take you twice as long to stop. It is important to know how to utilize front braking as well as how to keep your brakes in great condition. Refer to the following YouTube videos for a visual guide:

How To Brake Like A Pro – Road Cycling by Global Cycling Network

Basic Bicycle Repairs: How To Adjust Bicycle Front Brakes by expertvillage

Comfort Braking

Braking will slow you down, obviously, requiring you to spend more energy getting back up to speed later. Many cyclists instinctively engage in "comfort" braking when going down a steep descent. This can be costly in time and energy expenditure so I recommend paying attention to your braking practices.

One way to "break" this habit is to slow down to a speed where you feel comfortable, then analyze the path in front of you. As long as the surface appears safe and there are no obstructions ahead, you really don't need to brake further. Keep this in mind if you're a chronic brake-fiend. You can train yourself to ride safely while embracing a faster descent and enjoying the thrill ride.

Master Cornering

Cornering, the process of biking around a corner, is important to cyclists. Like braking, you will need to corner safely but the art is in minimizing the amount of time and momentum you lose in the process. Here is the process of cornering, broken down into discrete steps:

1. Shift down as you near a turn.

2. Stop pedaling and lean into the curve.

3. Coming out of the curve, stand and begin to pedal.

4. Pedal fast to regain your momentum before shifting back up to cruising speed.

Choose Your Gear Wisely

Experts may find it easy to shift gears and can wax eloquent on the subject, but beginning riders usually find all those gears and sprockets confusing. Here's what you need to know about shifting gears:

- First off, the bike has to be moving in order to shift gears. This may sound totally obvious, but the immediate application is that when you anticipate coming to a stop, you will want to shift down to an easier gear while you're slowing down. If you wait until you've stopped, it'll be too late.

- Most bikes have three gear cogs in the front, called chainrings. The chainrings are located at your pedals. You switch between chainrings using the **left** gearshift lever. This lever controls the front derailleur which moves the chain left or right to a different chain ring, depending on which set of cogs you choose to use.

- The **right** gearshift lever controls your choice of the cogs located at your rear wheel. Once you have selected a front chainring, you can easily stay there and just shift up and down the gears in the back as needed.

- Use your left gearshift lever when you need to make a big change in gears. For example, if you're approaching a hill and need to make a major downshift, it's easiest to accomplish this with a change in your front sprocket.

- Speaking of hills, approach a hill in the smallest chainring and the largest three back sprockets. If you find this super-easy, begin to shift, one rear gear at a time, until you can still make adequate progress without totally exhausting yourself in the process.

- It's easier to shift up than to shift down, so err on the side of lower gears.

- If you find you are in too difficult a gear in the middle of a hill, it's okay to turn and ride sideways across the road to get an easier pedal as you shift down to a better gear. Just don't impede traffic in the process.

- Use your right gearshift lever when you need to fine-tune your ride. It is designed to let you make gradual changes, as opposed to the massive adjustments provided by your front chainring.

- Whenever you start using a different bike, I recommend finding a fairly unused stretch of road and riding back and forth while you practice changing gears until you are comfortable with using the gearshift mechanism. You don't want to put off learning this until you're climbing a hill and discover it's steeper than you imagined and you need to quickly downshift to an easier gear.

- Avoid pairing your smallest front chainring with the smallest back gear; likewise, don't match up your largest front and rear cogs. This puts the greatest sideways force on your chain which can actually wear out gear teeth and misshape the chain links. Over time, this can result in rather annoyingly loud noises whenever you shift gears, a warning that you need a replacement chain, if not some new gears.

It will take time and practice to master the use of multiple gears, but as you gain strength, you will be able to choose your gears more accurately. You will find yourself tracking your progress by how quickly you can get up to speed.

Increase Your Functional Threshold Power

Functional Threshold Power, or FTP, is a key cycling term. It describes the fastest pace you are capable of sustaining for an hour. This provides an accurate measure of your performance fitness. Interval training can help build your threshold power. You will learn about some useful interval training programs in the next chapter. For now, it is important to learn how to measure, evaluate, and increase your threshold power.

First, you'll need to know your current FTP. You accomplish this by performing a power test. Your Functional Threshold Power is measured in watts by purchasing a power meter. Alternatively, you may use laboratory testing to get your results but this option is less popular and much more complicated, not to mention expensive.

You will use the results from your FTP test to begin planning your interval training. These results can also be used to pinpoint and address areas that are not up to par. After training for at least six weeks, perform another FTP test and compare it to the original numbers to see areas of progress and tailor future training.

Continue To Learn

Keep reading and learning about cycling. Stay alert to new research results that can help you improve your speed and endurance. Keeping informed can help you stay ahead of the game and work from the best information available.

Hire A Coach

If professional, competitive cycling is something you definitely want, consider hiring a professional cycling coach. Following the advice in this book can help you optimize your skills but a professional coach can take you to the next level, from reading to reality. While your training plan may be great, a professional coach can help you make it even better. Even if you just become 2% better, it means you're 2% better than other cyclists out there, and that gives you a 2% advantage.

You should only considering hiring a coach if you're serious about cycling, as these coaches can come with a hefty price tag. You'll want to make sure this is something you're willing to invest money in. However, the results can be significant; you can find yourself cycling at a much higher level, with the help of a good coach.

Chapter 4: The Top 5 Cycling Workouts

Having a well-balanced training regimen is crucial for developing the body you will need in order to reach your cycling goals. You can break down a solid cycling training program into three areas: speed, strength, and endurance.

Number One: The One-Hour Strength Hill Workout

This workout helps you build strength by utilizing the resistance of an incline. For this workout, you will need to find a hill that takes you about two minutes to climb. Start out with a moderate, 15-minute warm up session. You will complete this workout six times: twice sitting, twice standing halfway, and twice standing fully.

If you're a beginner, only complete this workout three times – once sitting, once sitting halfway and once standing – until you've built enough strength to perform two repetitions in each position.

Rep #1: Using moderate resistance, stay fully seated and pedal your way uphill. Return to the bottom by pedaling downhill in an easy gear.

Rep #2: Using increased resistance, stay fully seated and pedal your way uphill. Return to the bottom by pedaling downhill in an easy gear.

Rep #3: Using moderate resistance, stay fully seated and pedal your way uphill. Halfway uphill, stand until you've reached the top. Return to the bottom by pedaling downhill in an easy gear.

Rep #4: Using moderate resistance, stay fully seated and pedal your way uphill. Halfway uphill, switch to a more difficult gear and stand until you've reached the top. Return to the bottom by pedaling downhill in an easy gear.

Rep #5: Using moderate resistance, stand fully and pedal your way uphill. Return to the bottom by pedaling downhill in an easy gear.

Rep #6: Using a more difficult resistance, stand fully and pedal your way uphill. Return to the bottom by pedaling downhill in an easy gear.

To complete this workout, continue riding using a moderate gear for 30 minutes. Cool down during the last five minutes in an easy gear.

Number Two: Leg Strength and Speed Workout

This workout targets your quads, glutes, hamstrings, and hip flexors, everything you will need to master the strength of your pedal stroke. We will utilize jumping exercises to help train your legs for speed. The best time to begin this workout is at the end of your transition period. Once you are a month into this workout, you can begin to work toward maximum strength. By the time spring rolls around, you can stop the maximum strength workouts and just focus on the original exercises.

Strength Exercises

One Legged Pedaling – Begin with this exercise as it is an important part of the workout and can also serve as a warm-up exercise. This exercise is best performed on a stationary bike. Begin by placing both feet on the pedals. Start pushing with only one leg and let your other leg travel effortlessly with the other pedal. Pedal for one minute with each leg. Start with two sets of a minute each and build up to three sets of two minutes each.

Box Squats – This exercise requires a power rack and a box. The box should be tall enough that you can sit on it with legs bent at a right angle. Start out by standing in the power rack with the box set up behind you. Step under the bar and position it behind your shoulders. Squeeze your shoulder blades and pull your elbows forward. Take the bar off the rack and create a tight arch in your back.

Move your feet into a wide stance. Keeping your core muscles tight, lower your body until you're able to sit down on the box. Pause to let your hip flexors breathe. Push off the floor with your heels and feet to raise yourself to the starting position. Start with two sets of 15 repetitions each and work your way up to five sets of 50 repetitions each.

Leg Press – This exercise requires leg press equipment. Begin by sitting at the machine, placing your right leg on the platform and setting your left foot on the ground. Extend your right knee fully to unlock the weight and reach the starting position. Flex your hip and knee to lower the weight as far as your body allows. When you've lowered the weight as far as possible, hold it, then extend your knee slowly, returning to your starting position. Complete five sets of five leg presses for each leg.

Leg Curls – You will need a leg curl machine for this exercise. Lie face down on the machine, keeping your chest flat on it and your hands around the grips. Position the back of your ankles against the pads. Your knees should be aligned with the rotating cam. Without moving your hips from the bench, curl your legs up, squeeze them at the peak and then lower them back down. Start with two sets of 15 repetitions and work your way up to five sets of 50 repetitions.

Jumping Exercises

Squat Jumps – Stand with your feet shoulder width apart. Lower your body into a squat position and then explode upward into a swift, vertical jump. Land with right foot forward and left foot back, lowering into a lunge. Start with two sets of 10 repetitions, alternating lunge direction, and work your way up to five sets of 15 jumps

Pick three days a week to perform this workout, letting your body rest and recover during the off days. Complete this workout until around the fall. Begin with few repetitions and work your way up over a month to a moderate set of repetitions. For six months, complete this workout at maximum strength, then start scaling back to a more moderate, maintenance level.

Number Three: Half-Hour Speed Workout

This workout helps you focus on building speed. You can perform this workout either indoors or outside. Begin with a 15 minute workout at moderate resistance. To perform this workout, follow this pedaling schedule:

- Sit fully and pedal hard at a difficult resistance level for 10 seconds.

- Change to easier resistance and pedal for one minute.

- Change to a difficult resistance level and pedal hard for 20 seconds.

- Change to easier resistance and pedal for one minute.

- Change to more difficult resistance and pedal hard for 30 seconds.

- Change to easier resistance and pedal for two minutes.

- Change to more difficult resistance, stand, and pedal for 15 seconds.

- Sit down and pedal at an easy resistance level for one minute.

- Change to more difficult resistance, stand, and pedal for 20 seconds.

- Sit down and pedal at an easy resistance level for two minutes.

- Change to a moderate resistance level, sit down, and pedal for five minutes.

- Change to an easy resistance level and pedal for five minutes.

Number Four: Interval Endurance Workout

This workout can help your body build up aerobic endurance at a moderate to difficult resistance level. This workout can also be performed indoors or outdoors. Begin with a five-minute warm-up by cycling at an easy resistance. Change into a moderate gear and pedal into a slow rhythm for 15 minutes. After,

Change back to a lighter resistance and pedal for 10 minutes. Follow this with another 15 minutes of moderate resistance pedaling.

Number Five: Stationary Endurance Workout

This workout utilizes a stationary bike to help you build endurance using a changing Rate of Perceived Exertion. The great part about this workout is that you can adjust it from beginner to expert level. Depending on the level, it can take anywhere from a half hour to a little over an hour.

Step 1: Begin with an easy level of resistance and casually cycle for five minutes to warm up. For beginners, this is often labeled level 1. For advanced cyclists, this is usually labeled level 3 and for expert cyclists, level 5.

Step 2: Change the resistance to moderate and bike at a hard pace for five minutes. Beginners should bike at level 3, advanced at level five and experts at level 7.

Step 3: For the next three minutes, bump up your current level by three and continue to cycle while decreasing your level once each minute.

Step 4: Change the resistance to a moderate level and bike at a hard pace for five minutes. Beginners should bike at level 3, advanced at level five and experts at level 7.

Step 5: For the next three minutes, raise your current level by four and continue to cycle while decreasing your level once each minute. Beginners should start at level 7, advanced at level 9 and experts at level 11.

Step 6: Change the resistance to moderate and bike at a hard pace for five minutes. Beginners should bike at level 3, advanced at level five and experts at level 7.

Step 7: Beginners should immediately transition into the cool down phase. Advanced cyclists should repeat steps 2-6 and then go into a cool down phase. Expert cyclists should repeat steps 2-6 twice and then begin their cool down.

Designing Your Own Workout

There are many great cycling workouts in addition to these. Workouts are not always a "one size fits all" deal, so you may choose to design a workout based on your own needs. When you create your own plan you can more easily work it around your schedule. In this section, you will discover how to design your own cycling workout.

Step 1: Organize your training. I recommend using a calendar to break down your training seasons. The first step is to set both the start and the end of your training season.

Step 2: The second step is to establish a clearly defined goal. Consider how you can pursue this goal within your calendar. For example, if your goal is to win a specific race you can mark down the date of the race, creating a visual of just how long you have to prepare. If your goal is to strengthen your leg muscles, then you know to focus more on physical strength routines and not as much on actual training on your bike.

Step 3: The third step is to map out training rides, detail by detail. You'll want to include the hours you plan to spend on your bike, how many races you'll run, how often you'll bike for fun, and when you'll provide break and recovery time. Calculate the total number of hours per month you plan to spend on training and break those hours down across the calendar months.

Step 4: Break your monthly training hours into weekly hours and then into daily hours. If you want to spend six hours in the first week of the month on training, you could plan three one hour training sessions during the week and then a two hour casual ride over the weekend. Carefully include a recovery period every two weeks in which you reduce the amount of hours you budget to train.

Step 5: Review your custom workout plan each month. Periodic adjustments may be necessary. For example, if you reach your goal of training your leg muscles earlier than planned, modify your schedule to include more training sessions on your bike and less focus on physical strength exercises. Reviewing is important; the more consistently you train, the more your body will change.

Chapter 5: Proper Diet and Strength Training

While genetics play a small role in how successful you are as an athlete, a strategic diet and strength training program can help you become a master cyclist. By itself, cycling can help you maintain a healthy lifestyle, but without the right nutrition and amount of strength, it can actually cause a decrease your performance. An ideal nutrition plan for a cyclist includes foods that have the right balance of fats and carbohydrates to provide his or her body with energy. In this chapter, you will discover more in-depth information about the proper diet for a cyclist as well as how to include strength training to build your body up to peak performance.

Carbohydrates

Carbs are the best source of energy for cycling. Your body consistently burns carbs through cycling as well as your normal activities so it is very important to provide your body with a diet high in carbohydrates. More carbohydrates = more energy. It is important to avoid simple carbohydrates (white bread, candy, etc.) and aim for complex carbohydrates. These carbs can be found in fruits, vegetables, and whole grains.

Before a ride, enjoy a **pre-ride snack** loaded with complex carbohydrates. Simple ideas include a cup of fresh fruit, a whole grain bagel covered with peanut butter, or a piece of whole wheat toast. This snack will ensure enough fuel in your body to cycle for up to an hour. After an hour you'll want to replenish your carb levels if you're still riding. Sports drinks with electrolytes or an energy bar are a good choice. If you have reached your destination by this point, you can eat a meal loaded with carbs. A rule of thumb for refueling: provide your body with 30 to 40 grams of carbohydrate for every half hour you ride past 60 minutes. You should also rehydrate by drinking at least one full bottle of water or sports drink every hour.

Here are some great complex carbohydrate sources :

- Leafy green vegetables

- Kale

- Broccoli

- Cauliflower

- Onions

- Bell Peppers

- Apples

- Bananas

- Berries

- Tomatoes

- Avocados

- Citrus Fruits

- Whole Wheat Bread

- Whole Wheat Pasta

- Oats

- Bran

- Rye

- Beans

- Rice

- Potatoes

Proteins

Protein is a nutrient your body needs to function at peak performance during cycling. Lacking protein, your body will break down your muscles for energy, which can erase the hard work you've put into building your muscles. For cyclists, protein is important because it slows your body's ability to digest food, preventing blood sugar spikes and dips. Protein helps your body stay alert and energized when you're running short on carbs. The amino acids in protein enable your muscles to naturally rebuild their tissues. They allow your immune system to strengthen itself and help your body create white blood cells to fight off infection.

An ideal daily dosage of protein of protein for cyclists is half a gram per pound of body weight. For example, a rider who weighs 170 pounds would benefit from 85 grams of protein a day. You should eat roughly 20% of your daily protein intake within an hour of finishing a ride, in order to fuel your recovery. The best proteins for this purpose are from lean sources. Complete protein sources containing the full complement of amino acids, will help your body recover after a ride. Lean beef, dark-meat chicken, and fish are excellent protein sources that come packed with other valuable nutrients including iron and omega-3 fatty acids.

Fats

Fats sometimes get a bad rap in the world of nutrition because people mistakenly believe all fats are unhealthy. While saturated or Trans-fats are indeed unhealthy, you can actually boost your metabolism by judicious use of healthy fats. These fats can help you ride longer and they delay hunger pangs because it takes your body a while to digest them. The ideal healthy fat intake for an average cyclist is about 55 grams per day. Some examples of healthy fats include avocados, olive oil, almonds, other nuts and nut butters, flaxseed, tofu, salmon, tuna and the occasional piece of dark chocolate.

Strength Training for Cyclists

While strength alone will not necessarily make you a faster cyclist, it can load your body with important benefits, including a strong posture, general overall strength, and minimizing the chance of injury. Strength training can prevent you from losing muscle mass. Cyclists naturally focus on training the lower body, since strong legs are what power you forward. However, throwing some core exercises into the mix can benefit your upper body and sustain both proper posture and a well-coordinated whole body.

When you begin a strength training program for cycling, you will start by performing two to three sets of exercises and slowly progress to three or four sets. You should gauge any weights so as to be able to complete 12 repetitions in a set without strain. When five repetitions become effortless, you may increase the weight. If you find you cannot perform the correct set of repetitions with the weight you've chosen, back down to a lighter weight. Once you've been on this program for a few months, you can increase the amount of weight you use and reduce the number of repetitions, in order to build additional strength.

Strength Training Exercises

Squats – This exercise focuses on your glutes, quadriceps, and core muscles. Start by standing with your feet hip width apart and your hands at your sides. Push your hips back and lower your body as far as possible by bending your knees and forcing your body weight onto your heels. Balance yourself by holding your arms in front of you. Never squat so low that your knees reach out past your toes. Pause in the squat and then slowly return to a standing position.

Jump Squats – This exercise works your glutes, hamstrings, and quadriceps. Start by standing with your feet hip width apart and your hands at your sides. Lower yourself into a basic squat. From a squat, engage your core muscles and jump straight up. When you land, sink back down into the squat.

Box Jumps – This exercise focuses on your glutes, calves, hamstrings, and quadriceps. Place a box on a non-slip surface and stand at least three inches behind it with your feet hip width apart. Make sure your feet are parallel and facing forward. Bend your knees, swing your arms behind you, and make an explosive leap onto the box. Try to land on both feet. Stand up fully and then step down.

Leg Presses – This exercise focuses on your quadriceps, hamstrings, and glutes. Sit down on a leg press machine. Place your feet flat on the platform, hip width apart. Hold onto the support handles and slowly push your feet down on the platform until they are fully extended but not locked. Flex your knees and gradually lower the platform.

Deadlifts – This exercise works your hamstrings and lower back as well as your upper back, arms and shoulders. Stand behind a bar with your feet slightly farther than shoulder width apart. Your toes should be pointing forward. Using a hook grip, bend your knees slightly and grasp the bar a little outside of your legs. Keep your head up and your chest out. Breathe in. Straighten your legs and exhale as you raise the bar past your knees. Rest the bar against your thighs for a few seconds before slowly returning it to the ground.

Kettle Ball Swings – This exercise works your glutes, hamstrings, along with your back and shoulder muscles. Begin by standing behind a kettle ball with your feet shoulder width apart and your toes pointing slightly outwards. Squat down and grasp the weight. Stand straight up. As you squat again, swing the kettle ball back between your legs. Once it is behind you, rise up and thrust your hips forward so the kettle ball swings up and forward. Let it swing as high as your chest. Allow the ball to swing down between your legs as you begin another repetition.

Step Ups – This exercise works your glutes. You will need a small bench or stable chair that will create a 90-degree angle with your knee when you put your foot on it. Begin by placing your right foot flat on the chair and stepping up onto it. Step back down, starting with your right foot and following with your left. Take 15 steps up, alternating lead feet.

Split Squats – This exercise focuses on your glutes, quadriceps, hamstrings, back and abs and requires the use of a bench. Stand in front of the bench. Take one step forward with your right foot and place the ankle of your left foot on the bench. Take one or two hops forward to widen your stance. Lower yourself into a squat. Squeeze your leg and core muscles as you rise out of the squat. After performing this exercise for several repetitions, switch legs and repeat.

Lunges – This exercise focuses on your glutes and leg muscles. Stand straight with your head up and your shoulders back. Take one step forward and lower your body with your hips until your knees are at a 90-degree angle. Your front knee should be aligned with your ankle. Push up through your heels and return to your original position.

Side Lunges – This exercise focuses on your hips, glutes, and thighs. Stand with your feet and knees together and hold two dumbbells in your hands. Take a giant step with your right foot to the right to create a wide stance. Push off with your right foot and bring your leg back in to complete the first repetition.

Pendulum Lunge – This exercise works your hamstrings, glutes, calves, and quadriceps. Stand with your feet shoulder width apart and hold two dumbbells in your hands. Step forward into a lunge, step back out of the lunge and then immediately step into a backward lunge. For a more advanced workout, don't pause between the forward and backward lunge.

Russian Twist – This exercise works your core muscles. Sit on the floor and lean back 45 degrees from the ground. Keep your back straight, your head up, your knees bent and contract your abs. Reach your arms out in front of you. Without moving your lower body, twist your arms back and forth.

Barbell Rows – This exercise targets your upper back and your arms. Place a bar on the floor in front of you. Bend over and grasp the bar in an overhand grip. Keeping your upper body horizontal, pull the bar up against your lower chest and then lower it back on to the floor. Perform five sets of five lifts.

Side Bends – This exercise focuses on your abdomen and back. Stand up straight with your feet shoulder width apart and a dumbbell in your left hand, hanging down to your side. Place your right hand at your waist. Bend at the waist to the right as far as you can while keeping your back straight and breathing in. Pause and breathe out, then rise back up to your starting position. Repeat this exercise to the left.

Back Extensions – This exercise works your lower back. Lie face down and extend your arms above your head. Tighten your abs to create a small space between the ground and your stomach. Lift up your left arm and right leg; stretch them out as far as possible. Hold for five seconds and then return to your starting position. Repeat, lifting your right arm and left leg.

Crunches – This exercise works your abdomen. Lie on your back and point your knees toward the ceiling. Put your hands behind your head, pointing your elbows slightly up. Tuck your chin and curl your upper body so that your head and shoulders raise off the floor. Hold this position for a couple seconds before releasing.

The Anatomy of A Strength Training Program

Your strength training program is designed to be adjusted as your body, and its training needs, change. Strength training is designed to fill the gap between active road seasons, sustaining and enhancing your muscles in the interim.

Anatomical Adaptation Phase

You should begin this phase between one and two months before you start off-season training and after you've ended your active season. This phase prepares your muscles for an increase in both workload and exertion. It consists of two to three exercise sessions per week for six to eight weeks. The best exercises to engage in during this phase are squats, deadlifts, lunges and bodyweight exercises such as pushups. You should complete each set of exercises three to five times with 20 to 25 repetitions per set. Allow your body to rest for one to two minutes between sets.

Maximum Strength Phase

You can begin the maximum strength phase when you begin to base build. This phase can increase muscle fiber strength and build a core body support system for your major muscle groups. The maximum strength-building phase should last three to six weeks.

Exercise once or twice weekly during this phase. Most importantly, ease into your work. Begin with light loads and work your way up steadily, preparing your body for even more heavy lifting. During this phase you will want to focus on squats, dead lifts, Olympic lifts, and squat presses. Complete three to five sets with four to six repetitions each. Rest your muscles for three to five minutes between each set.

Muscle Endurance Phase

Begin the muscle endurance phase toward the end of your maximum strength training. You are now focusing on your aerobic metabolism. Cyclists who need to pedal at high RPMs for several hours at a time will benefit most from this phase.

You will be priming your body to perform greater repetitions while reducing recovery time. This phase should last six to eight weeks. You will complete one to two sessions per week. You will focus on squats, lunges, planks, pushups, and other exercises that work your core muscles. You should perform each set two to four times with 20 to 30 repetitions per set. Give your body 60 to 90 seconds of rest between each set.

Strength Maintenance Phase

During the strength maintenance phase you will sustain the strength of your upper body while giving your lower body a rest. You can utilize this phase of training throughout the season, except for weeks when you have a race. You will perform these exercises once a week. Strength maintenance exercises include planks, pushups and other exercises that focus on working your core muscles. Complete two to three sets with 10 to 15 repetitions per set, resting for one to two minutes between each set.

Chapter 6: Mental Strength Techniques

Impulses and Choice

It is not uncommon for cyclists to lose their cool in the heat of competition, especially toward the end of a race. Frustration is the strongest trigger for loss of self-control. When frustrated, it is easy to forget the rules and forego the niceties of fair play and etiquette. Regrettable actions often follow.

While you can't control a frustrating moment, you *can* control the way you *respond* to that moment. For example, let's say you are cut off by another cyclist. While you have no control over your natural – and normal – impulse of anger, how you respond to this event is up to you; it's your choice to be nice or nasty, to respond with grace and professionalism or petty vindictiveness.

This is where the mental part of the sport enters the picture. How you respond in that moment of frustration is largely determined by how you have trained your mind to think. Yes, mental training is every bit as important as your physical workouts, hence the focus of this chapter.

Ya Gotta Be Tough

To be a successful cyclist – or a successful anything, for that matter – you must nurture the quality that allows you to dig deep inside and keep on keeping on, even when (and especially when) things seem beyond hope of recovery. I call this mental toughness. Mental toughness can help you become a powerful cyclist. It will prevent you from being easily discouraged by the weather, swayed by others or derailed by your own emotions. Mental toughness sets you free to respond with positive creative energy to the most challenging of circumstances.

Mental toughness is a function of <u>confidence</u> combined with a solid self-awareness and a healthy sense of pride. It stems from a commitment to one's given, or chosen, work and is strongest when we are acting to help others, as part of a group, a team, or a community.

The Component Of Inner Pride

The first component of mental toughness is your ability to acknowledge your successes internally and be nourished the sense of sheer goodness that stays behind afterwards. It matters little whether anyone else notices your accomplishment; actually, it can lend you the greatest satisfaction when your success is overlooked. But *you* know. And you bask in the warmth of that knowing.

The most successful – and the happiest – individuals in the world are those who are able to experience that inner pride in a job well done. They recall personal triumphs that have contributed to their formation as a person. The significance of these triumphs lends a settled weight to one's living and forms a solid foundation from which to face life's vicissitudes.

Reflective Activity

In order to begin to build your inner pride, you will need to practice periodic reflection of your life. This doesn't have to be a major production; many people find it helpful to just take a little time at the close each day to reflect on the events of the day. You won't see anything notable unless you look, so sit yourself down, and walk your thoughts through your day. Look for things that went well and things that went not so well. Did you beat your personal record in your daily ride? If so, allow yourself to feel all the goodness of that accomplishment. Did you complete a workout with energy to spare? Bask in your level of fitness. Enjoy it for all it's worth.

Periodically, allow your mind to wander further back through your life. Often we won't recognize the significance of life-changing choices until much later, so as you meander through your days look for successes that you perhaps didn't notice at the moment but have made a big difference in the way you live today. For example, let's say six months ago you made the decision to walk the dog every day. How is your life different now as a result? Are you more relaxed? More fit? Is the dog? Look for the good and celebrate it.

It's also valuable to record your accomplishments so you're reminded of them later. Choose something that will trigger your memory of an accomplishment, find a way to represent it, and serve as a periodic reminder. Some people journal their successes and review their journals on a regular basis. Others post a picture or pick up a piece of driftwood as a visual reminder. You can also write a description on a three-by-five card and post it somewhere you'll see it every day. Do whatever works for you. The important take-away is to help yourself remember to think of your successes as a true and good part of who you are.

The Confidence Component

Confidence is a function of preparation, practice, and problem solving. In your workouts and physical training sessions you are **preparing** your body for the rigors of riding well. You **practice** key skills, repeating them over and over again – hundreds of times if necessary – until they happen naturally. Then you make contingency plans: you shift your mind into **problem-solving** mode and visualize, one at a time, each thing that can go wrong, rehearsing a scenario until you are satisfied you know what to do no matter what happens. You can't stuff confidence into yourself by sheer will-power; you first learn to perform flawlessly, and then confidence naturally follows.

Building Confidence

So, what if you really lack confidence? What if you see yourself as a bumbling idiot, a clumsy klutz, a complete failure? In this case, you have your work cut out for you, not because of how lame you are, but because of how lame you *think* you are! But fear not (we'll address fear, too, in a moment); you can indeed reverse your lack of confidence.

Since confidence comes as a result of skill mastery, the easy way to begin to build genuine confidence is to develop a skill. Choose something you don't know how to do yet. Notice that word, "yet?" That's how you need to start viewing your inabilities, as something you just haven't gotten around to mastering...yet.

As I said, select something you don't yet know how to do. Make it something fairly simple; it needs to be a straightforward skill you can learn in a short amount of time. Set your sights on mastering this skill, I mean, really dive into learning it. Overlearn it, if such a thing is possible. You want this skill to be so well ingrained that it becomes second nature.

When you've got it well-mastered, you can then tell yourself, "Look at me! I'm not a failure. I just learned to do thus-and-so!" And so you have. You've completed one stepping stone on the path to confidence. Whenever in the future you start to feel like a failure, hold that new skill up before your eyes and remind yourself that you have something significant that you have learned to do. Then go on and pursue another skill. Before long, you'll start to realize you have all sorts of skills. You'll also start to notice skills you already have but you hadn't noticed them before, because you either didn't think they were valuable or you just hadn't paid attention to them.

Here are some additional tips to increase your confidence:

Reflect on Positive Experiences. Many people with low self-esteem tend to wallow on negative past experiences. By thinking about times when you felt great, you can use those examples to push forward into the future. For example, think about a time when you made a great accomplishment in improving your leg strength. Remember how good it felt and what you did to get there. Your chances of feeling more confident in the moment can increase. It's also a good idea to make a journal and record of all your favorite positive experiences throughout your life. You can include pictures, awards, events, friends, or anything that makes you happy. Then, be sure and read through this journal a couple of times a week to keep your spirits high.

Use Your Body Language. Your body language communicates. If you slump and appear weary, you give your competition hope of beating you. Slumping and sagging can open the door to a defeatist attitude. Conversely, positive body language can improve your outlook on life and can actually give you a confidence boost when you need it. By carrying yourself with correct posture you can fool your mind into thinking you are in great shape. Imagine how you great you look and give yourself a smile that you can feel down to your toes!

Don't Take It Personally. When it comes to sports, it is common for athletes to feel hurt by comments from peers or coaches. Any criticism is doubly painful because it seems to strike at the heart of who we are, not just at how we perform. However, there is much to be gained from criticism, if we are able to separate it out from our sensitive egos.

Yes, a negative criticism can hurt. It can seemingly strike at the heart of what is most important to us. However, much of the sting can be removed by accepting a few key truths:

- I live by the knowledge I have, which is always limited. Therefore, I will always be vulnerable to the criticism of others who know (or *think* they know) more than myself. This is nothing to be ashamed of. Instead, it's a wonderful opportunity to grow and learn.

- Even if a criticism is not wholly valid, it will have some truth to it; learn to discard the irrelevant and focus on the truth you can benefit from.

- And the hardest for me: learn to see beyond words that cut and destroy to the truth behind them. Choose not to accept and react to the tone of voice, but instead absorb what is useful to your life.

- Express appreciation for what you've learned from the criticism. This allows you to consciously set aside what hurts you and affirm what is good.

I've found that when someone says something critical to me, they are usually just trying to help me. When I worked in retail my boss would give me plenty of feedback, most of which really hurt because it seemed to always center on some personal weakness or failure. Because it hurt my feelings, I would take her comments personally. I knew deep down inside that she was just trying to help me improve, but that didn't always determine how I felt.

If a person is being critical of you, especially a mentor or coach, remind yourself it's not because of who you are. Assume the criticism is given so that you can improve your performance. Train yourself to think of criticism as a positive opportunity to grow and learn.

Relax and Focus

This is a great exercise to refresh yourself when you feel tired. It doesn't take long, and can be done almost anywhere.

Let your eyes relax into a soft gaze into the distance. Focus your mind on each sense in turn, first what you feel on your skin, then shift your attention to the smells around you. After you have absorbed the smells, retain your awareness of them as you shift your awareness to the sounds around and in you. Gradually add in the sights, noting the shades of color, the light, and the shadow.

Select A Success Mantra

Personal success mantras are a great mental technique for all athletes and they really do work! The best part about mantras is that they are you create them yourself; you tailor them to speak to your own needs.

The majority of us, by nature it seems, will default to a negative mantra when we mess up. For example, if you trip on the carpet how likely are you to instinctively respond with, "I'm such a klutz"? Even though that phrase may sound trivial, it's still negative. Personal success mantras work to undo all those negative messages by focusing on positive ability statements. They give you credit for your positive abilities and skills. Examples of success mantras are: "I am smart and know how to handle my bike in traffic," "I am increasing my physical strength," or "I am eager to face and master cycling challenges."

Your mantra can be phrased anyway you'd like, as long as it is a statement of positive ability. Motivation experts recommend you word your statements in the present tense (e.g., "I am smart..." not, "I will be smart..."). They also recommend you use the adverb, "easily" to show that this is a well-mastered ability (e.g., "I *easily* climb hills").

The next step is to get into the habit of saying your positive personal success mantras many times over the course of a day. You should speak a mantra aloud. If you are in a place where you can't speak aloud, whisper it to yourself. If this is not possible, silently mouth the words as you say it inwardly.

Create frequent reminders to speak your mantras to yourself. Write them down on paper and post them on your bathroom mirror, put them on your phone and set alarms to remind you to repeat them, Post them in your closet, in your car, and near your work computer.

You can use specific activities as triggers to repeat your mantras to yourself. I use the start of my drive time as a trigger. Others use break times including bathroom breaks as a trigger. You can use any activity that is frequently repeated as a trigger to repeat them. Let your mantras be the first thing you say in the morning and the last thing you say to yourself at night.

Positive Self-Talk

Self-talk is an important tool but only when it's positive. Positive self-talk has been proven to drastically boost your self-confidence. The most successful cyclists use positive self-talk because it works!

Negative self-talk can easily tear down hope within seconds. A major step in building positive self talk is increasing our awareness of our own negative speech. Your sensitivity to negative self talk will grow as you increase the positive self talk in your life.

If you find yourself overwhelmed by the sheer dominance of negative messages in your mind, here is one way to defang and defeat them. For one day, commit to writing down every negative thought (or as many as possible). This will be an inconvenience, since you'll need to stop whatever you're doing to write things down, so expect the day to be full of interruptions. Carry a pad of paper and a pen, with which to jot down each negative thought.

At the end of the day, put your pad down and give yourself a good night's sleep, then pick up the pad again in the morning, along with a separate piece of paper. As you review each statement, think of how you could reword it into an opposite, positive statement and write that positive statement on your sheet of paper. For example, if you think, "I'm terrible at hill climbing," you can replace the word "terrible" with "awesome." Instead of sending yourself a discouraging message, you've chosen to infuse yourself with something you *can* do!

It's amazing how a simple word change can alter your attitude. If you think you're awesome at hill climbing, then you'll probably be more excited to do it! Even if you don't really believe yourself at first, that's okay. Keep repeating that statement. Over time, something inside you will begin to accept that yes, we do an awesome job of climbing hills. Your attitude toward yourself will have changed, and for the better. This will spill over into other areas. You will find you have greater confidence in your ability to tackle other mundane – but necessary – parts of life.

Visualization

Visualization is a powerful technique. It can help you reverse years of negative thinking. It can give you greater confidence in your ability to reach your objectives. It can train you to think like a winner.

What is the next performance hurdle you want to achieve? Imagine what your life will be like once you've achieved it. You can choose a small hurdle, such as your next training ride, or a huge goal like winning the World Cycling Championship. Walk through the details of the event, visualize yourself overcoming with ease each challenge, difficulty, or danger along the way. Imagine how great you'll feel when you accomplish your objective, how it will change your life, and what possibilities this achievement will open up for you in the future. That is the essence of visualization.

Your visualizations will be built around your individual cycling goals and what you need to do to reach them. The top pros in the world use visualization to help them in their pursuits, and you can, too. Make visualization a daily habit to dramatically increase your chances of success.

The Power of Visualization

Let's look at a famous example to see just how effective visualization can be. Long before he was famous, actor Jim Carrey used to park his car by the "Hollywood" sign in Los Angeles and imagine what his life would be like when he made it big. He even wrote himself a huge check and dated it for five years in the future. Sure enough, well before the five years were up, he was paid $10,000,000 for his work in the movie *Dumb and Dumber*.

If visualization can inspire somebody like Jim Carrey, imagine how it can help you in *your* life! Still not convinced? Let me give you a little science. Scientific research has shown that your brain cannot tell the difference between reality and things you imagine. This means that when you visualize, your brain experiences it as reality and stores as memories whatever you have "experienced" as part of your visualizations. Your memories inform your beliefs, and your beliefs tell you what you are capable of achieving. So, when you visualize, you are imbedding real possibilities in your mind, making it easier to believe good about yourself.

Visualization Tips

Include all of your senses in your visualization. Imagine what you'll hear, the feel of your bike under you, the smells along the route. Taste your energy drink as you hydrate yourself and feel yourself growing stronger in the process. All along the way give yourself a feeling of calm confidence and superior strength. Picture yourself completing your event with ease. Imagine how you'll laugh and what you'll do to celebrate at the end. Really submerge yourself in your vision. Make it as real as possible.

Visualize your accomplishment from different angles. See yourself as if you were in a movie and you are in the lead role. Picture yourself through your own eyes, reaching out to achieve your dreams. Then view the event through the eyes of your best friend. Imagine it as if you were reading a book, a book written in the third-person. If you can think of any other eyes to picture it through, do it.

Go "Live" with your dream. Dress, walk, and talk as if you have already achieved your goal. When you put on your cycling togs, visualize yourself as having just won a race and preparing to be crowned the champion. When you're cooling down at the end of a ride imagine you've just crossed the finish line; let yourself feel all the emotions that go with winning. Whatever you want to accomplish, start living and acting like you already own it. Live as if you have the confidence of a winner, and you may well find yourself thinking and believing you *are* a winner!

Pair up your personal success mantra with mental images. Say things to yourself that you can imagine others saying about you, once you've got it made. State your positive affirmations from different viewpoints as well.

Watch from a distance. Visualize your accomplishment as if you were watching it from ten to fifteen feet away. Just allow the scene to flow naturally with you doing everything perfectly to achieve the desired goal.

Turn your visualizations into physical reminders. Put together a collage of your dreams using pictures of yourself or clipped images from magazines or the internet. Hang up inspirational quotes in your workout area. Set a success trigger image as your screen saver.

Comment on inspiring internet stories and share them with friends. Better yet, post online your own latest achievements and pay attention to your friends' affirming responses. Review these whenever your enthusiasm flags or you've had a rough day; they'll remind you to believe in yourself.

Overcome Fear

Fear can have deadly effects on your cycling career. While it is natural to have some fear, for example, feeling nervous before your first big race, uncontrolled fear can cause you to lose focus, self-confidence, and motivation. Having the abilities to display ultimate self-confidence and to conquer your fears is a sure way to get you on the fast track to cycling success. While these two areas are difficult for some cyclists to achieve, they are definitely not impossible.

Fear is a part of our being when we are born and stays with us until death. This self-preservation reaction keeps us safe, but it can also impede us from our success. Everyone has fears. It is how you deal with them that matters. Fear has a tendency to keep you stuck where you are and does not allow you to progress any further in your development until the fear is overcome.

Someone who is afraid of lightning and thunder will continue to be afraid of it if they don't do something about it. They might hide in a closet or under their bed until the storm is over. They might miss an event like a family reunion or an outing with friends merely because there is supposed to be bad weather. This person is stuck and can easily miss out on enjoyable events as long as they give in to the fear. In a cyclist's case, fear of failure may prevent you from participating in a big race or from cycling at all.

Techniques for Overcoming Fear:

Yoga is a perfect tool to address panic and fear. It promotes good posture and builds strength, both of which are perfect for cyclists. Yoga is a combination of breathing and movement. It is an ancient practice that melds together the body, mind and spirit. Breathing is very important in Yoga because it prepares the brain to be calm. The different stretches and poses of yoga center the body and make it stronger and more balanced.

Another part of Yoga is meditation. Meditation is used to link the spirit to the mind and the body. Many practitioners run thorough a litany of mantras and positive affirmations while meditating, posing, and breathing; this can reinforce confidence and overcome fear. When you do your exercises, repeat your personal success mantras to banish fear. The repetition of the mantra wriggles into the subconscious mind and you might find yourself gravitating toward what you used to fear with no problems at all.

Breathing

Breathing exercises help you relax and focus in a way that can overcome pain and calm your fears. Deep breathing slows the heart rate, relaxes muscles, and aids in concentration. It centers on the diaphragm, the muscle that runs across the bottom of your lungs. It is this muscle that a singer uses to project the most power and to finesse vocal control. This is what you use almost instinctively when you are powering down the road.

Diaphragmatic Breathing Exercise

This exercise is designed to help you become aware of your diaphragm and to train you to breathe from your diaphragm, without tensing other muscles unnecessarily.

Before we begin, you should be wearing clothing that is loose around your midsection, to allow for freedom of movement. Start by lying down on your back. This exercise can be performed on the floor or on your bed. It is also a good exercise to use when you first wake up in the morning, because it gently increases your circulation even before you get out of bed.

Notice how your body naturally breathes. When you inhale, notice how your belly button rises and your waist area generally expands outward. As you take air into your lungs, they expand. Since your ribcage is rather restrictive, all that air has to go somewhere, so your lungs expand downward, stretching the relaxed diaphragm muscle and pushing down all the organs that reside below it.

To a count of five, exhale all of your air, squeezing out every last drop. Notice how your belly lowers and everything seems to be pressing upward into your ribcage. That is largely the work of your diaphragm.

Hold this tension with your "gut muscles" but keep everything in your neck relaxed. Now, on a count of eight, relax and begin to fill your lungs with air. Still keeping everything in your neck relaxed, allow your belly to expand as you load your lungs as full as possible. Hold this fullness as you breathe in once more. This breath allows the upper lobes of your lungs to fill; you may actually feel some stretching across the top left and right sides of your chest, just below the shoulder bones.

Hold this a couple seconds as you pay attention to how each part of your body feels, then release and let your body relax as you exhale.

Let your body rest and breathe comfortably. Notice that when you are not thinking about your breathing, your body naturally breathes diaphragmatically. There is no clenching of the neck, no tightening of the vocal cords.

This is how you want to breathe when cycling, as well as for the rest of your life. If you feel your neck muscles tensing, or if you clench your airway shut, these are signs of tension, and are often your body's instinctive response to fear.

Turn Your Head

It's pretty hard to turn your head when you're clenching your neck or vocal cords. One simple way to remind your body to relax from the neck up is to simply turn your head to the left, then to the right. You may need to do this a couple times, but your body should get the message and relax those muscles, allowing your lungs and diaphragm to do the work of breathing without further interference.

Cooling Breath Exercise:

This breathing exercise draws air across the tongue, creating a cooling sensation that calms the nervous system. I recommend doing this whenever you feel fear rising..

1. Start by sitting comfortably.

2. Stick your tongue out and curl up its sides, making it into a tube.

3. Raise your chin and point it toward the ceiling.

4. Inhale through your curled tongue.

5. Hold your breath for a few seconds, then relax your tongue and let it slide back into your mouth.

6. Exhale through the nostrils, then lower your chin.

Repeat this action six times at first, but you may increase to 12 repetitions over time. The more you practice it, the more this exercise will imprint on your brain. Eventually, this will become an automatic response to fear

.

Tensing Exercise

This is a good exercise to practice when you become aware that you are anxious or afraid. When fear strikes, your muscles tense up involuntarily. In this exercise, you will tense your muscles beyond any existing tension. Then you will consciously relax them, in the process, letting go of the physical grip of fear.

Ideally, you will perform this exercise when lying down, but this can be modified to use when seated or standing, wherever you are when you identify tension as a physical effect of fear or anxiety.

1. Breathe in deeply, using your diaphragm.

2. While you hold your breath, tense the muscles in your head, neck and shoulders and count to 10.

3. Let your breath out slowly and force the muscles in your neck to relax, followed by your shoulders, your upper back, and then your upper arms. Focus on how each part of your body feels when the muscles are relaxed.

4. Now inhale deeply again, keeping your head, neck and shoulders relaxed. This time, tense your upper arms, followed by your lower arms, your wrists, hands, and fingers. Pay attention to how each tense muscle feels, and then relax each muscle group gradually, beginning with your upper arms, then moving down to your lower arms and your hands, all the way down to the tips of your fingers. As you relax each muscle group, absorb how the relaxed muscles feel.

5. Proceed to the trunk of your body beginning with your upper chest, moving down and around to your back, working down your ribcage to your belly and again around to your back, visualizing your inner organs tensing and relaxing as you move downward toward your hips.

6. Take another deep slow breath as you continue from your hips and buttocks down to your thighs, your lower legs, your feet, and ultimately, to your very toes.

Practice these exercises once a day and use them whenever fear takes hold. They will help slow your heart rate and will allow you to move the fear from your instinctive muscles to the more rational part of your brain that can process and choose how to respond to the threat.

Bring Out The Balloon

If your fear seems to automatically kick you into racing-heart, fast-breathing panic, you might want to try this trick. Keep an uninflated balloon in your pocket. Whenever panic starts, whip out your balloon and start blowing it up. This will stop the panicked breathing and can help your muscles relax and flex normally. It also helps pull your mind together to focus on the task at hand.

Besides, what's more fun to play with than a colorful balloon? Once it's fully inflated you can play a song with the whistle as it deflates, or you can tie it off and bat it around. If that's too silly, you can just give it to the first child – or adult – you see, turning your panic into creative generosity.

The Component of Ownership

Another attitude behind mental toughness is the idea of owning my life. This doesn't exclude the input of other people; it just acknowledges that this life has been given to me as a sacred trust. The choice is mine as to how I live it.

If you own your life, you will not just drift along but you will proactively take initiative to build the kind of life you think is valuable. You will periodically review where you are in your life and will make course corrections to keep heading toward your destination.

Goals help you achieve success, not just in cycling but in life. Your goals provide a roadmap for your dreams. Without them, you may very well wander off into the woods and spend the rest of your life there.

Define Your Dream

Where do you want to go with your cycling? Do you want to be able to ride with your spouse? Keep up with your kids? Do you want to be able to safely and effectively navigate to work and back? Or is your dream to make the professional circuit? Whatever your dream is for cycling, it's important that you clearly define what you want; otherwise you won't know what to do to get there and my easily find yourself wasting time and effort better expended elsewhere.

I suggest you take some time right now to think through exactly what it is you want to accomplish. Write it down. This will be your starting place for the rest of the work we will do to get you there.

Dreams express your desire. Goals help you head in the right direction. Plans tell you in detail how to go about reaching your goals.

Set Goals

Goals strengthen your motivation. They make it possible to actually start out in one direction and end up where you wanted to go in the first place. They give you something to aim for and help you sustain your focus in a single direction.

Now that you know where you're headed, it's time to set down your goals. Take some time right now to write down what you need to work on now that can take you toward your dream. Don't stress out over your goals; this is simply a starting point. As you see the need, your goals can always be adjusted, tweaked, and rewritten to better suit your needs. I'll walk you through the process of defining your goals in the next paragraphs, but for starters here are some general guidelines to help you:

- Describe, in measureable terms, specifically what you want to accomplish.

- Set a target date for completion of your goal. Since tasks expand to fill the amount of time allotted to them, a target completion date will keep your goal from extending on indefinitely.

- Decide how you will celebrate and reward yourself when you reach this goal. Sometimes the achievement alone is enough motivation to sustain you to reach your goal. But if you find your motivation flagging, a reward to look forward to can make the difference between fading out and persevering to the end.

Let's walk through the process of developing a goal. For example, let's say your original goal states, "I will easily complete my workout." Okay, that is a goal, but it's not specific enough. What do you mean by the word "workout"? A workout could mean anything, as in "Well, I walked one mile today so that's my workout." No, it needs to be specific enough that you can tell when you've achieved it.

It's time to dig deeper. Pretend you have a coach who is telling you this is your goal. Imagine your coach saying, "You will easily complete your workout." Are you just going to nod your head and reply, "Okay"? Probably not, because you'll need more information.

If you had a coach, at this point you would probably be asking, "What defines my workout ? Am I working out my entire body or just certain parts?" This could lead your coach to reply with, "You will easily complete your lower and upper body workouts."

Now you know specifically which parts of your body you're working out. While your goal is much clearer, it still lacks enough detail to know if you've completed it. I would ask my coach, "How often will do this?" Let's pretend your coach replies with, "You will easily do your lower and upper body workouts two times a week." Okay so now we have a specific area of the body and a measurable number but I still see more information that can be broken down.

My next question would be, "How many times during those four sessions a week would I work out each body part?" My coach could reply, "Work your lower body twice a week and your upper body twice a week," to which I would reply, "Which four days should I use?" My coach might reply, "Monday and Wednesday for your lower body, Tuesday and Thursday for your upper body."

At this point, the revised goal states, "I will easily complete my lower and upper body workouts four times a week, working my lower body on Mondays and

Wednesdays and working my upper body on Tuesdays and Thursdays." Now we have a clear and specific goal. I know what I am working out and when.

Though I think I would be satisfied with this goal, I could go even deeper and specify what times of the day and where I will do this. If I included those details, my goal would read something along the lines of, "I will easily complete my lower and upper body workouts four times a week in my home gym, working my lower body on Monday and Wednesday mornings before breakfast, and my upper body on Tuesdays and Thursdays before breakfast."

Here are the iterations our sample goal has taken:

- I will easily complete my workout.

- I will easily complete my lower and upper body workout.

- I will easily complete my lower and upper body workout four times a week, working my lower body on Mondays and Wednesdays and working my upper body on Tuesdays and Thursdays.

- I will easily complete my lower and upper body workouts four times a week in my home gym, working my lower body on Monday and Wednesday mornings and my upper body on Tuesdays and Thursdays, all before breakfast.

Which goal do you think will be most successful? That was just one example. Make your vision compelling and something that really excites you. Too many people set small goals that lack passion; don't be afraid to dream big and shoot for something truly incredible.

I could make one more modification to make this goal complete. I will add a phrase to tell me when I have reached my goal. Sometimes goal completion can be stated in terms of a specific date, as in the date of a race you wish to compete in. In this case, however, I have decided that my goal will be reached when I can pedal through a two-hour race without needing to stop and take a rest.

The completed goal now reads, "I will easily complete my leg and upper body workout four times a week in my home gym, working my lower body on Monday and Wednesday before breakfast, and my upper body on Tuesday and Thursday before breakfast, until I can pedal through a two-hour race without needing to stop for a rest." Now that's what I call a truly complete goal!

Filling In the How Tos

Once you have clearly defined a goal, the next step is to develop an action plan. An action plan helps you with the details of reaching your goal; it fills in the "how tos."

If I don't have a home gym, what can I do to find a place for my workout? Setting up the logistics may entail researching gym memberships in my area or investing in the purchase of gym equipment for my home.

Since I stated that I wanted to complete this workout before breakfast, I would need to arrange my schedule accordingly. If I start work at nine a.m. and I eat breakfast at eight, instead of getting up at seven to get ready I may have to set my alarm for six a.m. If I plan to get up at six, I will need to go to bed by ten p.m. the previous night, in order to get adequate sleep.

This is an illustration of another tactic you can employ to plan the necessary action steps to accomplish a goal. This works particularly well if you are working toward a specific date. Simply start with the end date in mind and work backwards, deciding what needs to be accomplished before that date – in reverse order – in order to prepare for the deadline.

The key is to work out all the logistical details ahead of time so you can focus in the moment on actually accomplishing the task at hand. If I don't take these preparatory steps, then I probably won't be successful in working out consistently and my dream of a successful two-hour ride will be delayed even longer than originally planned.

Set Milestones

For particularly large goals, you may find it easier to break them down into smaller sub-goals, or milestones. For example, if I want to be able to pedal for two hours without needing to stop to rest I might set a first milestone of being able to pedal for 30 minutes without stopping. After reaching that milestone I would focus on increasing my successful pedal time to 40 minutes, then an hour, etc. Those smaller accomplishments not only help make my progress visible but also help to sustain my motivation as I measure my growth.

It is not possible to achieve a huge goal overnight so breaking it down into smaller sub-goals can be a great help. I find that when I complete small milestones it motivates me to press on toward my end goal.

Contingency Planning

Since cycling can be intensive and high impact, it is important for cyclists to have a contingency plan in the event of an injury or an otherwise unexpected event. Pre-planning for unexpected events can condition you to automatically respond, minimizing any sudden decrease in performance. All sorts of unexpected scenarios can occur, from a sudden injury to your bike chain breaking. The best way to face these unplanned events is to have an back-up plan prepared for execution. No matter what, you can learn to be prepared to face any situation.

The most common unexpected scenarios for cyclists are when you get tired or dehydrated during a ride or race, when something on your bike breaks, when you incur an injury, when the weather goes wrong or when you've lost or forgotten a piece of equipment. Luckily, most of these situations only require a quick fix.

Tiredness and dehydration can be prevented by stashing plenty of high protein snacks and drinks in your backpack or a bicycle travel compartment. Carrying a poncho or other protective gear answers for the weather. It's also advisable to travel with some money. You know what they say; money buys everything.

If something on your bike breaks during a ride, there's no need to freak out. By traveling with a small repair kit you can travel prepared for any equipment failure. Most repair kits include screwdrivers, patches, a small air pump, wrenches, and other repair tools that frequently come in handy. Bike repair kits are compact so you can easily take them with you.

Fully charge a cell phone and carry it with you. A phone can be a literal life-saver in emergencies. If you're traveling through a sparsely populated area, your cell phone may not get reception, so it won't hurt to carry a few survival tools like a lighter or box of matches, a knife, and a small mirror with which to draw attention.

It can be a real pain if you forget to bring key equipment. If you forget an essential piece like your helmet, you may have to scratch the ride. However, forgetting something that isn't critical to your safety, such as your gloves, isn't a show-stopper. You can always take a deep breath, remind yourself to pack them next time and carry on. If you're on a long ride it's always helpful to store extra equipment with a friend who lives nearby. I personally store my camping equipment at my grandparents' house because I know it will be safe there. My grandparents also live near a campground I frequent, which is perfect for my needs.

Finally, if the weather turns bad, there are steps you can take to deal with it. If you're riding and the sky opens up and dumps rain upon you, take shelter as soon as possible and just wait it out. If you enjoy a good rainstorm then take the time to appreciate it. I actually like to ride in the rain, if the weather is warm enough to be comfortable, the road is empty, and there's not a lot of lightning crisscrossing the sky.

Be Honest – With Yourself

As the popular phrase goes, "honesty is the best policy," and that couldn't be truer when it comes to cycling. Personal honesty can help you achieve the results you want and drop methods that aren't getting you anywhere. If your workout routine is not helping you achieve your goals, then feel free to change it up.

This is also true for other techniques. If a personal success mantra doesn't really help you, exchange it for something that better fits your personality and needs. The only energy you should be spending is figuring out which techniques and workout routines will give you the best results.

Chapter 7: Inspirational Biking Stories

The Story of Lance Armstrong

Lance Armstrong is probably the most well-known name associated with cycling. This athlete has competed in hundreds of races and chalked up many wins, including seven Tours de France.

As a child, Armstrong was into athletics, competing primarily in swimming and triathlons. By the age of 16, Armstrong was already regarded as a professional triathlete; he was named champion of the National Sprint Course triathlon in 1989 and 1990. From 1992 to 1996, Armstrong was part of the Motorola Cycling Team. He was named winner of the World Race Championship in 1993, he competed in the 1996 Olympics, and he won his first Tour de France victory in 1999. By the age of 25, Lance Armstrong had established himself as a successful athlete and his name had become a household word.

In 1996, two months after signing on with the French cycling team Cofidis, Armstrong was diagnosed with testicular cancer. The cancer had already spread to his lungs and his brain. Cofidis promptly dropped him from their team.

After surgery, doctors doubted he would survive, but Armstrong moved his cancer treatment to Indianapolis where he received a targeted mixture of chemotherapy drugs that was able to successfully combat his cancer. By February of 1997 he was cancer-free and ready to return to cycling. Lance Armstrong celebrated his return by winning the Sprint 56K Criterium in Austin, Texas.

Before long, he was invited to join the US Postal Team. Just three months after being declared cancer-free, Armstrong could be found training in the Appalachian terrain of North Carolina. That year he finished fourth place in the Vuelta a Espana race and won a second Tour de France. Armstrong proved himself a major contender, successfully riding against most of the established professionals in the world of cycling. He continued to compete until his retirement in 2011.

Even though he was ultimately stripped of his achievements because of performance-enhancing drug use, we can still learn from the man's unwavering determination in his fight against cancer. His tenacity ultimately led to a breakthrough cancer treatment, allowing him to beat the odds and survive to ride again.

Greg LeMond

The story of Greg LeMond begins before that of Lance Armstrong, but as you will see, the lives of the two are intertwined. LeMond's star shone brightest in the 1980s. He won three Tours de France and two World Championships. He was the first American to win the Tour de France and with Armstrong now stripped of his medals, remains the only American to hold that honor.

Like Lance Armstrong, Greg LeMond also suffered physical setbacks and overcame them to ride again. Early in the year after he won his first Tour de France, LeMond broke his wrist in a race. After returning to America, he was shot and almost killed in a hunting accident. About that time LeMond also learned he had mitochondrial myopathy, a rare disease that saps muscle strength.

It was a long two years before he would compete again, but Greg fought his way back, winning the Tour de France followed by the World Championship, a rare cycling accomplishment. The year was 1989. The following year Greg LeMond won his third and final Tour before retiring from the world of racing.

Ten years later Lance Armstrong's star was rising. Along with it rose LeMond's awareness of the widespread doping that was going on behind the scenes. However, as a former star, whose records the new challenger was now breaking, it would appear like so much sour grapes if he were to blow the whistle. He mostly withheld comment or offered a neutral reply. Once, however, he mentioned that if Lance were declared clean it would be, "the greatest comeback in the history of sports," but otherwise, "it would be the greatest fraud."

That was all it took for the cycling world to write him off. He was disinvited from cycling events and Trek chose to end a lucrative partnership with Greg, which had provided a major source of his income. Thus began what LeMond terms "12 years of hell."

After being pushed out of the spotlight, Greg and his wife Kathy were able to get down to the business of living. For Greg, it was a time of physical and emotional healing and a chance to spend more time with his family. During that time, Greg was able to come to grips with, and ultimately share with others, that he had been sexually abused by a family member when but a child. In going public with his painful past, Greg stated that if only one person is helped by his example, then it is worth all the pain he has suffered over the years. Both he and Kathy have since become involved in the organization 1in6, a California nonprofit that provides support to the one in every six men statistically who have been sexually abused as children.

With the Trek partnership dissolved, the LeMonds also had to figure out how to make a living. They set to work, designing an innovative line of carbon fiber racing bicycles. These days, Greg and Kathy LeMond are doing well. Greg's anti-doping stance has been vindicated and they've emerged from the cloud of their dark days to a fresh enjoyment of life. Theirs is a story of perseverance in the face of injustice and building new dreams atop the ashes of past pain.

The Story of Marshall Taylor

Marshall Walter "Major" Taylor was the fastest cyclist in the world, holding that title for six years. This is quite an accomplishment in an age when bicycle racing was the hottest sport in America. And Taylor was the hottest thing in cycling! He literally blew away the competition. The real kicker? He was an African American, competing under the added weight of what he called "that dreadful monster prejudice" in the era of Jim Crow, lynch laws, and segregation.

Taylor was born in 1878. His father was a coachman for a wealthy family in Indianapolis. The family had a son the same age as Taylor and the two became close friends, to the point that Taylor was invited to live in their home and was treated as part of the family.

When Taylor was 12, the family gave him his first bicycle, which he learned to ride and went on to teach himself complex tricks. Word of his skills got around and before long he was hired to put on trick riding exhibitions outside a local bike shop. Because he often wore a military uniform for these exhibitions, he earned the nickname "Major."

That same year, Taylor ran and won his first amateur race. Two years later, he broke the amateur track record, twice, but this didn't set too well with the owners. They ultimately banned him from the track.

Marshall moved to Worcester, Massachusetts with his boss and manager, Louis Munger. There he trained and raced on Munger's cycling team. During his first professional race, he beat out several other professional riders in the final heat. Not long afterwards, he took first place in yet another professional race. By 1898, Taylor had won the vast majority of his races and held seven cycling records.

At that point, Taylor had earned the right to be named National Champion but a new league had formed, complicating his claim to the title. One year later, however, he won the world championship again, becoming the first African American – and the second black man in the world, behind boxer George Dixon of Canada – to gain the title of World Champion in any sport.

As time went on, Taylor competed throughout Europe and as far as Australia, but he continued to suffer threats and roughing up by other cyclists, along with curses and nasty epithets from the American crowd. He was treated so badly in the South that he eventually stopped competing there entirely.

All the while, Marshall Taylor continued to carry himself as a gentleman, never responding to the threats or fighting back against mistreatment. He countered everything by winning, and by winning big. He became a huge favorite of the fans, to the point that promoters found it necessary to allow him into races, regardless of how they felt about letting a black man ride. He also became the first African American celebrity athlete, earning more than $34,000 in peak years, a huge sum for the day. He was wealthy, compared to most athletes, black *or* white. Marshall Taylor paved the way for other athletes of color, setting an example for all people to emulate.

Conclusion

I hope this book was able to help you to learn more about becoming a better cyclist, improving your workouts and your nutrition, increasing your biking skills and gleaning inspiration from some of the greatest cyclists in the sport.

You can become a great cyclist. All it takes is time... and a commitment to training. Professionals review their dietary and nutritional habits to ensure they are consuming the right balance of carbs, proteins, and fats to keep their bodies energized for the road. They perform strength training and targeted workouts to shape their bodies into the optimal cycling physique.

Your next step is to figure out where you are as a cyclist and how far you want to take your cycling. Do you ride for fun or do you have hopes and dreams of becoming the next Greg LeMond? Whatever your objective, you can start by reviewing your health habits, your performance strengths and weaknesses, and then by setting goals accordingly.

Review your eating, sleeping, and workout habits using the guidelines in this book to ensure that your body has adequate energy, and that you're working the correct muscles to help you cycle to success. Then, look to the areas you need to improve. Are you good at speed but need to build up your strength and endurance? Are your hamstrings and quads fully built up but you need to work on your glutes? Use the tips you have discovered here to design your own plan to take you from where you are now to achieving your own dream of success! And of course, be sure to have some fun doing it!

Finally, if you discovered at least one thing that has helped you or that you think would be beneficial to someone else, be sure to take a few seconds to easily post a quick positive review. As an author, your positive feedback is desperately needed. Your highly valuable five star reviews are like a river of golden joy flowing through a sunny forest of mighty trees and beautiful flowers! *To do your good deed in making the world a better place by helping others with your valuable insight, just leave a nice review.*

My Other Books and Audio Books
www.AcesEbooks.com

Popular Books

BASEBALL
BASEBALL STRATEGIES

THE TOP 100 BEST WAYS TO IMPROVE YOUR BASEBALL GAME

ACE McCLOUD

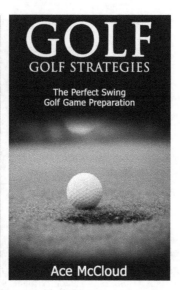

GOLF
GOLF STRATEGIES

The Perfect Swing
Golf Game Preparation

Ace McCloud

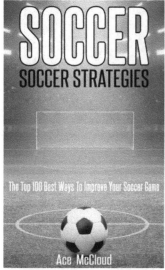

SOCCER
SOCCER STRATEGIES

The Top 100 Best Ways To Improve Your Soccer Game

Ace McCloud

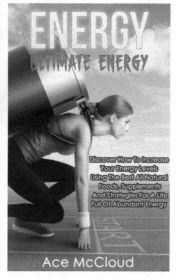

ENERGY
ULTIMATE ENERGY

Discover How To Increase Your Energy Levels Using The Best All Natural Foods, Supplements And Strategies For A Life Full Of Abundant Energy

Ace McCloud

FOOTBALL
FOOTBALL MADE EASY

BEGINNER AND EXPERT STRATEGIES FOR BECOMING A BETTER FOOTBALL PLAYER

Ace McCloud

MOTIVATION
MASTER THE POWER OF MOTIVATION TO PROPEL YOURSELF TO SUCCESS

Ace McCloud

LOSE WEIGHT

THE TOP 100 BEST WAYS
TO LOSE WEIGHT QUICKLY AND HEALTHILY

Ace McCloud

SELF DISCIPLINE

Unleash The Power Of Self Discipline,
Influence And Willpower In Your Life
To Achieve Anything

Ace McCloud

Ace McCloud

HABIT

The Top 100 Best Habits
How To Make A Positive Habit Permanent
And How To Break Bad Habits

ATTITUDE

Discover The True Power Of
A Positive Attitude

Ace McCloud

ULTIMATE HEALTH SECRETS

HEALTH

Strategies For Dieting, Eating Healthy, Exercising,
Losing Weight, The Mediterranean Diet,
Strength Training, And All About Vitamins,
Minerals, And Supplements

Ace McCloud

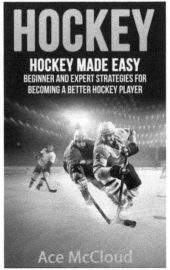

HOCKEY

HOCKEY MADE EASY
BEGINNER AND EXPERT STRATEGIES FOR
BECOMING A BETTER HOCKEY PLAYER

Ace McCloud

Be sure to check out my audio books as well!

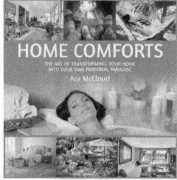

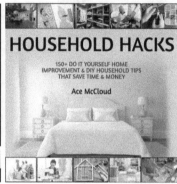

Check out my website at: www.AcesEbooks.com for a complete list of all of my books and high quality audio books. I enjoy bringing you the best knowledge in the world and wish you the best in using this information to make your journey through life better and more enjoyable! **Best of luck to you!**